WALKING IN FAITH

The Peter, Paul, and Mary Principle

ENDORSEMENTS

This book is so important, and Dr. Craig is the brilliant thinker and servant required to deliver it.
—**Dallas Jenkins**, Creator, The Chosen

First of all, your book is POWERFUL! Just wow! It's a faith boost as it is looking at Jesus and our walk with him from a different angle and taking us to a new dimension. As soon as I started reading it, I started diving into a new faith ocean and was impacted by the extraordinary story telling power. As you read this book, you are going to be challenged and your faith will be boosted beyond your expectations. Get ready for a baptism of faith.
—**Isik Abla**, TV host, author

Like a secret key to a hidden treasure, *Walking in Faith: The Peter, Paul, and Mary Principle* unlocks the mystery to God's supernatural goodness influencing our hurting world through his people.
—**Beth Patch**, Senior Editor at CBN.com

Faith is the currency of heaven. Without it, we cannot access all God has for us. In *Walking Faith: The Peter, Paul, and Mary Principle*, Dr. Craig von Buseck stirs and challenges faith in the life of believers that causes the impossible to become possible. Be empowered as you read!
—**Tom & Jane Hamon**, apostles, Vision Church, Christian International

Years ago, I read a little book about faith and the unconditional love of God called *Favor: The Road to Success*. That anointed book set me on a path to fulfilling God's call on my life while impacting the lives of people around the world through my writing and speaking. Now Craig von Buseck has written a new book I believe will have

a similar impact on the lives of its readers. In *Walking in Faith: The Peter, Paul, and Mary Principle*, Craig shares a biblical key that can unlock the door to walking in your God-given calling and to reaching hurting people around the world with the love of Jesus. It's a must-read!
—**Michelle Medlock Adams**, award-winning author of more than 100 books, including *They Call Me Mom* and *Springtime for Your Spirit*

In his latest book, *Walking in Faith: The Peter, Paul, and Mary Principle*, author Craig von Buseck gives us encouragement for walking out our faith. Through his foundation of biblical knowledge, he examines the lives of three biblical characters, giving today's believers valuable insight. Truly a great book for our time.
—**Edie Melson**, award-winning author and director of the Blue Ridge Mountains Christian Writers Conference

Walking in Faith: The Peter, Paul, and Mary Principle by Dr. Craig von Buseck is a must read for any Christian who truly desires to experience a new level of faith in their walk with Christ. Dr. von Buseck is a master writer and brings the Scripture alive through the lives of the apostle Peter, apostle Paul, and Mary, the mother of Jesus. Each chapter will stretch your faith in a good way. As you read this faith-building book, pray before you begin each chapter, and ask the Holy Spirit to give you the special gift of faith that you will learn about. Then as you read, expect faith to rise up within you to see God do the impossible through you for his glory. I have read many books on faith, but Dr. von Buseck does something unique that stirs my faith to a new level. You will not be the same after reading *Walking in Faith: The Peter, Paul, and Mary Principle*, by Dr. Craig von Buseck.
—**Daniel B. Gilbert, Ph.D.**, assistant professor, Regent University School of Divinity, President of EmPowered Living Int'l Ministries & Bible Schools

Craig's new book is a most worthy read! Take the time to invest in reading this faith builder and you'll find newfound strength and inspiration amidst the turbulent times in which we live.

—**Larry Tomczak**, best-selling author, cultural commentator, and board member of Intercessors for America

This book will not only encourage those who are new to the faith of Jesus Christ, but it will reassure those who have been on the journey for many years. We all need guidance in our walk; at least I do. And we all must make huge decisions throughout our life. This book will help provide inspiration for our choices. In our walk with the Lord, faith is essential as we: 1) receive salvation by faith, 2) receive a revelation of God by faith, 3) recognize truth of Scriptures by faith, 4) receive guidance from God by faith, 5) receive healing and protection by faith, 6) look for the Lord to return one day by faith. When we understand the Peter, Paul, and Mary Principle, we can grow in God's love and mercy. And that is what this book does so well. Great job and fantastic insight, Dr. von Buseck.

—**Del Duduit**, author

In his latest, revelatory read, *Walking By Faith: The Peter, Paul, and Mary Principle*, historical writer, award-winning author, teacher, encourager, and so much more, Dr. Craig von Buseck, takes the reader on an all too common (yet uncommon) topic of discussion, "walking by faith," and puts real and compassionate skin on it, with biblical heroes whose stories could be anyone of us—and are. Whether seasoned in your faith, a beginner, or still wondering if this "Jesus" is real at all, you will wonder no more and instead be blessed with the knowing that you too can truly "walk by faith"—spiritually, practically, and in every way. A great read … a needed read … a classic for the ages … and real hope for today!

—**Jensine Bard**, host, Testimony radio program

So often we read the Bible and wonder how it applies to our day-to-day lives. Dr. Craig von Buseck masterfully walks the reader through a relatively simple principle he discovered from his immense background of research and Bible study. The journey is a beautiful read to see how these faith-filled leaders walked out their beliefs and then transformed them into life-changing action. Even more relevant is how you and I may see the mind, body, and Spirit alignment for our own opportunities to live out this tangible and authentic principle every day. Dive in and experience it one faith decision at a time.

—**April Ballestero**, founder, One Light Ahead Strategic Leadership

WALKING IN FAITH

The Peter, Paul, and Mary Principle

DR. CRAIG VON BUSECK

A Christian Company
ElkLakePublishingInc.com

COPYRIGHT NOTICE

Walking in Faith: The Peter, Paul, and Mary Principle

First edition. Copyright © 2022 by Dr. Craig von Buseck. The information contained in this book is the intellectual property of Dr. Craig von Buseck and is governed by United States and International copyright laws. All rights reserved. No part of this publication, either text or image, may be used for any purpose other than personal use. Therefore, reproduction, modification, storage in a retrieval system, or retransmission, in any form or by any means, electronic, mechanical, or otherwise, for reasons other than personal use, except for brief quotations for reviews or articles and promotions, is strictly prohibited without prior written permission by the publisher.

Unless otherwise indicated, Scripture quotations are from The ESV Bible (The Holy Bible, English Standard Version.), copyright 2001 by Crossway, a publishing ministry of Good News Publishers. Used by permission. All rights reserved.

Scripture quotations labeled NLT are taken from Holy Bible, New Living Translation, copyright © 1996, 2004, 2015 by Tyndale House Foundation. Used by permission of Tyndale House Publishers, Inc., Carol Stream, Illinois 60188. All rights reserved.

Scripture quotations labeled NASB are taken from the (NASB®) New American Standard Bible®, Copyright © 1960, 1971, 1977, 1995, 2020 by The Lockman Foundation. Used by permission. All rights reserved.

Scripture quotations labeled NKJV are taken from the New King James Version®. Copyright © 1982 by Thomas Nelson. Used by permission. All rights reserved.

Scripture quotations marked (GNT) are from the Good News Translation in Today's English Version—Second Edition Copyright © 1992 by American Bible Society. Used by Permission.

Cover and Interior Design: Derinda Babcock, Deb Haggerty
Editor(s): Susan K. Stewart, Judy Hagey, Deb Haggerty
Author Represented By: Cyle Young Literary Elite

PUBLISHED BY: Elk Lake Publishing, Inc., 35 Dogwood Drive, Plymouth, MA 02360, 2020

Library Cataloging Data

Names: von Buseck, Dr. Craig (Dr. Craig von Buseck)

Walking in Faith: The Peter, Paul, and Mary Principle / Dr. Craig von Buseck

p. 184 . 23cm × 15cm (9in × 6 in.)

Identifiers: ISBN-13: 978-1-64949-602-7 (paperback) | 978-1-64949-603-4 (trade hardcover) | 978-1-64949-604-1 (trade paperback) | 978-1-64949-722-2 (e-book)

Key Words: Peter walks on water; Jesus walking on water; Saul on the road to Damascus; Angel Gabriel and Mary; Inspirational Study; Motivational; Holy Spirit

DEDICATION

To my sister, Erin von Buseck Staaf. Like Peter, you have weathered life's storms by keeping your eyes on Jesus. Like Paul, you have been knocked down, but you rose up and obeyed the call of God. Like Mary, you may not have always understood, but you responded to God's leading with, "Be it unto me according to your word." I am inspired by the way you continue to shine the light of Jesus in the darkness.

With much love.

TABLE OF CONTENTS

Dedication xi
Foreword xiii
A Note: the Telling of Bible Stories xvii
Chapter One—Faith: The Gateway to Heaven 1
Chapter Two—Peter: An Unlikely Hero of Faith 13
Chapter Three—Paul: A Detour on the Road of Faith 27
Chapter Four—Mary: A Shining Example of Faith 39
Chapter Five—Faith in the Life of Jesus 53
Chapter Six—Faith in Action 63
Chapter Seven—Faith for Salvation 79
Chapter Eight—Faith for Guidance 89
Chapter Nine—Faith for Provision 99
Chapter Ten—Faith for Healing 107
Chapter Eleven—Faith for Favor 115
Chapter Twelve—Faith for the Gifts of the Spirit 127
Chapter Thirteen—Faith for the Future 139
About the Author 161
Endnotes 163

FOREWORD

In two decades of counseling with families and couples, I've recognized the Christian life must be a grace-filled journey, following Christ and biblical truth amid our own imperfections and the challenges we all face. As we follow this path, it's comforting to know ordinary people from the Bible faced the same struggles we do and yet overcame and triumphed by walking in faith. It's also encouraging to know that God has given us principles in Scripture to guide us along the way.

In *Walking in Faith: The Peter, Paul, and Mary Principle*, my friend and colleague, Dr. Craig von Buseck shares a fascinating insight he discovered during a time of Bible study while considering three important encounters with heaven:

- Peter responding to the call of Jesus to walk with him on the water.
- Saul (Paul) encountering Jesus on the road to Damascus.
- Mary receiving the news from the angel Gabriel that she would bear the Christ child.

In these three scenarios, Craig uncovered a pattern of faith he has named the Peter, Paul, and Mary Principle.

In my practice, at Focus on the Family, and especially in my own family, I've seen the necessity for walking in faith. Understanding how to step out in faith is vital if we are to be obedient to God's direction for life. Often God calls us to attempt things that seem beyond our own strength and resources. Stepping out in obedience to this call requires a thorough understanding of what the Bible means when it says, "we walk by faith and not by sight" (2 Corinthians 5:7).

Today, we think of the biblical characters of Peter, Paul, and Mary as heroes of the faith and pillars of the early church. It's important to understand they were just ordinary people like you and me. But God called each of them out of their ordinary lives and into an extraordinary adventure with him (the first step in this principle). Being obedient to that calling required a step of faith.

In fact, being obedient to God's call could have cost Peter, Paul, or Mary their very lives.

Yet because of their love for Jesus, each of these disciples chose to leave the status quo behind, to step out of their ability and into God's ability. Each of them not only heard the call, but they acted boldly in faith. As a result, they not only received what God had promised, they were each launched on a journey that took them to places with Jesus that were beyond their wildest dreams.

This is the beauty of the Peter, Paul, and Mary Principle. Each of us has a ministry God has designed for us to fulfill. The Bible gives us amazing promises concerning God's plan for our lives:

> For we are his workmanship, created in Christ Jesus for good works, which God prepared beforehand, that we should walk in them. (Ephesians 2:10)

> Your eyes saw my unformed substance; in your book were written, every one of them, the days that were formed for me, when as yet there was none of them. (Psalm 139:16)

God has amazing plans for our lives, but like Peter, Paul, and Mary, we must do our part in seeing that plan become a reality. He invites us into his kingdom and calls us "God's fellow laborers" in the work of the gospel (1 Corinthians 3:9). Paul tells us we have been entrusted by God with the ministry of reconciliation—laboring with him as he reconciles the people of this world to himself through a plan of love (2 Corinthians 5:19).

The opportunities for God's people to shine the light of his love in this dark world are enormous—but so are the dangers. It will take a tremendous amount of faith and work to see the call of God fulfilled in your life. The Peter, Paul, and Mary Principle is a key that can help you unlock the doors to the supernatural life God intends for you as a disciple of Jesus Christ.

By understanding this important principle, like Peter, Paul, and Mary, you can go from the ordinary to the extraordinary through a steadfast faith in Christ, and then by taking the courageous and trusting leap into a world beyond your wildest expectations.

—**Dr. Daniel P. Huerta**, Vice President of Parenting and Youth, Focus on the Family

A NOTE:
THE TELLING OF BIBLE STORIES

I've always been a storyteller. I started spinning tales as a child to entertain my siblings and friends. Later, I'd weave stories into songs for my Christian rock band. God blessed me with a vivid imagination, and for that I am most grateful. As a senior in high school, I sat in the balcony at church and listened to the sermons with rapt attention. The words spoken by the pastor came alive, playing out the scenario like a movie in my mind.

While reading Scripture, I often 'see' the narrative unfolding in my mind's eye. This is the approach I have taken with the chapters in this book describing the scenarios of Peter's encounter with Jesus while walking on the water, Saul's encounter with Jesus on the road to Damascus (later Paul), and Mary's encounter with the angel, Gabriel, where she was called to carry the Christ child. While these three stories are based squarely on the divinely inspired Biblical record, I have given artistic interpretation of how the stories may have played out in ancient times.

Tyler Thompson and the other writers of the popular video series, 'The Chosen' use a similar approach in presenting the gospel narrative while adding artistic interpretation and literary license. "We have source material that's divinely inspired. Then we're exploring ways to look between the lines and explore the motivations of these characters, all in hopes that it would point people to Jesus or at least make them at a minimum curious, or bring to life some things they think they already know."

This is also my goal in retelling these Biblical narratives while employing artistic interpretation and literary license to paint word pictures for my audience. As you read these narratives I encourage you to also read the passages in your chosen version of the Bible – I'm a fan of the ESV, the NLT, and the NASB. As this book is primarily a Bible study, I pray that your love for God and His Word will be enhanced as you read these narratives of how real people encountered our loving Savior, Jesus Christ.

—CHAPTER ONE—
FAITH: THE GATEWAY TO HEAVEN

Jesus was impressed.

There weren't a lot of things that moved the creator of the universe to wonderment, but on this day, he marveled as he witnessed the faith of the Roman Centurion whose servant was near death:

> When he had entered Capernaum, a centurion came forward to him, appealing to him, "Lord, my servant is lying paralyzed at home, suffering terribly."
>
> And he said to him, "I will come and heal him."
>
> But the centurion replied, "Lord, I am not worthy to have you come under my roof, but only say the word, and my servant will be healed. For I too am a man under authority, with soldiers under me. And I say to one, "Go," and he goes, and to another, "Come," and he comes, and to my servant, "Do this," and he does it."
>
> When Jesus heard this, **he marveled** and said to those who followed him, "Truly, I tell you, with no one in Israel have I found such faith. ... And to the centurion Jesus said, "Go; let it be done for you as you have believed." And the servant was healed at that very moment. (Matt. 8:5–13, italics and emphasis added)

This Roman officer captured the attention of the Son of God. In all his interactions with his fellow Jews, Jesus had not encountered such an expression of confidence in his ability to miraculously heal the sick.

Jesus was impressed when people responded in faith. He marveled at it.

But we are also told he marveled at unbelief. Mark's Gospel gives the account:

> He went away from there and came to his hometown, and his disciples followed him. And on the Sabbath he began to teach in the synagogue, and many who heard him were astonished, saying, "Where did this man get these things? What is the wisdom given to him? How are such mighty works done by his hands? Is not this the carpenter, the son of Mary and brother of James and Joses and Judas and Simon? And are not his sisters here with us?" And they took offense at him. And Jesus said to them, "A prophet is not without honor, except in his hometown and among his relatives and in his own household." And he could do no mighty work there, except that he laid his hands on a few sick people and healed them. **And he marveled because of their unbelief**. (Mark 6:1–6, italics and emphasis added)

Jesus responds to both the expression of faith and the lack thereof with wonder. Notice the passage says, "He could do no mighty work there." These verses are essential to understand how biblical faith works.

FAITH IS ESSENTIAL

The Bible has much to say about faith.

> And He said to them, "...for truly I say to you, **if you have faith the size** of a mustard seed, you will say to this mountain, 'Move from here to there,' and it will move; and **nothing will be impossible to you**." (Matt. 17:20 NASB, emphasis added)

> Therefore, I say to you, all things for which you pray and ask, believe that you have received them, and **they will be granted you**. (Mark 11:24 NASB, emphasis added)

> And **without faith it is impossible to please him**, for whoever would draw near to God must believe that he exists and that He rewards those who seek him. (Hebrews 11:6 ESV, emphasis added)

Faith is an important spiritual key that opens the door to receiving from God. To experience the fullness of the abundant life Jesus promises to believers, it is vital we understand the spiritual gift of faith and how it operates in our lives. An important component of biblical faith is to understand that because we have a physical body and live on planet earth, there must always be a natural or material component to everything we receive from God in addition to the spiritual or soulish elements.

The apostle James speaks of this mysterious connection between faith and corresponding works when he writes:

> What good is it, my brothers, if someone says he has faith but does not have works? Can that faith save him? ... So also faith by itself, if it does not have works, is dead.
>
> But someone will say, "You have faith and I have works." Show me your faith apart from your works, and I will show you my faith by my works. ... You see that a person is justified by works and not by faith alone. ... For as the body apart from the spirit is dead, so also ***faith apart from works is dead.**** (James 2:14–26, italics and emphasis added)

At face value, this passage of Scripture would seem to contradict the writings of the apostle Paul that declare we are saved by faith and not by works. But the balance James is bringing is that in every aspect of our walk with God, there is a spiritual component (faith) and there is also a natural component (works). Paul tells us in Romans chapter ten that in our salvation experience there is the spiritual—faith and grace—and there is also the natural—confession with our mouth (more on this in chapter seven). The confession is the corresponding work that brings completion to our faith.

This is true not just in the salvation experience, but in every encounter of receiving from God.

Jesus himself demonstrated this principle. As a part of the godhead, Jesus is a spirit. But the Gospel of John tells us Jesus, the Word of God, became flesh, and dwelt among men (John 1:14) So also in every transaction with heaven, there is a spiritual element and a natural or earthly element—faith with corresponding works.

Without the earthly element, the spiritual element will not be fully effective. Faith is important, and corresponding works are also important. But the essential element in every interaction with heaven is the grace of God.

This is the essence of a pattern of faith I discovered during a time of Bible study. I call this the Peter, Paul, and Mary principle.

Now, I'm not talking about the famous folk trio who sang "Puff the Magic Dragon"—as great as they are. I'm referring to three biblical giants of the New Testament: the apostle Peter; the apostle Paul; and Mary, the mother of Jesus.

This pattern of faith is repeated in three different scenarios: when Jesus calls Peter to come to him on the water; when Jesus appears to Saul (later Paul) on the road to Damascus; and when Gabriel appears to Mary and announces she will carry the Messiah. I was amazed to discover in all three encounters the communication between God and humanity is the same.

I was astounded even further when I discovered this pattern is the same with us today—but we will unpack all of that in future chapters.

As we move ahead, it is helpful to remember a lack of faith will hinder God's blessing just as an expression of faith will allow his blessings to flow in our lives. To see God's plan fulfilled in our lives, we must understand the concept of biblical faith and how it works in our daily lives. The Peter, Paul, and Mary principle will help to make this concept clear.

Despite their weaknesses, their failures, and their shortcomings, these three human beings—Peter, Paul, and Mary—grew to become towers of faith. In each of these biblical stories, we will see normal people responding in faith and receiving the fulfillment of the promises of God. This pattern of faith and corresponding works is a key to unlocking the doors to the kingdom of heaven and receiving every promise God promises to us in this life.

These folks lived in perilous times when the witness of the church was critically needed to turn the world toward the light. As a result of the faith of these courageous believers, and thousands like them in those early days, critics of the time said of them, "These men who have turned the world upside down have come here also" (Acts 17:6).

The same can be true for us today if we will walk in faith and obedience to God's Word. We can see the world changed—and instead of upside down, it can be "turned right side up!"

What do you need in your life? Do you need wisdom, favor, provision, healing, guidance, protection, an increase in the operation of the gifts of the Spirit? A proper understanding of the Peter, Paul, and Mary principle can unlock the blessing of God in your life, in your family, in your church, and in your community.

People of Faith Must Arise

As it was in the early days of the church, we live in a time of growing darkness, where the body of Christ must rise, stand strong, and shine the light of biblical truth. As we approach the time of Christ's return, the evil in this world will grow darker, so the light of God's truth must shine ever brighter.

In the face of growing wickedness, the church must demonstrate God's compassion. In response to the hatred and cynicism, believers must exhibit the love and grace of Jesus. In the face of injustice and cruelty, Christians must take a stand for truth, justice, and compassion in this world.

When people in the world say there is no way—that the problems facing humanity are insurmountable—people of faith must rise up and declare that with God, all things are possible (Matthew 19:26).

Through Jesus and the Bible, God has revealed his compassion, love, grace, and plan for mankind. Now, as his representatives in the earth, we must arise and demonstrate God's love in tangible ways. This can happen practically through helping to alleviate the critical problems facing this world. In light of the perplexing difficulties we face today, this can only be done if God's people will seek him for the answers, and then by faith pull them from the spirit realm into the natural world.

Understanding the Peter, Paul, and Mary principle enables us to step out of our own ability and into the realm of God's supernatural power.

Giants of the Faith

These three biblical titans lived at the same time, but they couldn't be more different from one another:

- Peter was a salty-tongued, pig-headed fisherman who thought he knew more than the Son of God,
- Paul (Saul) was a highly-educated, silver-tongued legalist, who also thought he knew more than the Son of God, and
- Mary was a young Jewish maiden from the backwater of Judea who hardly knew anything about the world, but knew enough about God to respond, "Behold, I

am the servant of the Lord; let it be to me according to your word." (Luke 1:38).

They were three completely different persons, with completely different personalities, who had one thing in common—despite their shortcomings and human frailties, they responded to the call on their lives in faith with corresponding action and then received the promises made to them by God.

And through them, God changed the world, forever.

WHAT IS YOUR MOTIVATION?

We have already established faith is an essential component of the victorious Christian life. But let me be clear on this point—as Bible-believing Christians, we don't concern ourselves with receiving from God so we can gain riches or power merely for our own selfish pursuits. A proper, balanced view of faith is needed to walk out our lives in a manner pleasing to God and also effective in communicating God's love to mankind.

The proper ordering of these priorities can be seen in Jesus's answer to the question of what is the greatest commandment.

> You shall love the Lord your God with all your heart and with all your soul and with all your mind. This is the great and first commandment. And a second is like it: You shall love your neighbor as yourself. (Matt. 22:37–39)

Our priority must always be love of God first, and then, from that relationship, grace is given by God to help us truly love our neighbor.

In other words, it's not about me.

By applying the Peter, Paul, and Mary principle to our lives, we can learn to receive from God to become a channel of his love and provision to lost and hurting people. We can step into a place where we become a conduit of our Father's blessings to hurting people for the sake of his kingdom plan.

RECONCILING MANKIND TO GOD

The apostle Paul gives us God's perspective in 2 Corinthians chapter 5 as he explains we as disciples are called to the ministry of reconciliation. We serve as ambassadors of his truth and love to lost and suffering people. Receiving from God should never be only for the building of our own personal fortunes here on earth. It must always have a kingdom purpose.

Jesus made it plain we are not to store up for ourselves treasure here on earth, but we are to store up treasures in heaven.

> But lay up for yourselves treasures in heaven, where neither moth nor rust destroys and where thieves do not break in and steal. For where your treasure is, there your heart will be also (Matt. 6:20–21).

That doesn't mean we all have to take a vow of poverty either. God wants to bless his people, and that can include the material things we need and also want. He wants to meet our needs and even provide in abundance. Like any good father, he delights in giving us good and fun things to bring joy to our lives. But the ultimate blessing God wants to bring is a relationship with him—and then through that connection to become a channel of his blessings to others.

Why? Because he loves his creation.

God wants to bless us so we, in turn, can bless others in his name. That's why the prayer of Jabez is so powerful:

> Oh, that you would bless me and expand my territory! Please be with me in all that I do, and keep me from all trouble and pain!" And God granted him his request. (1 Chron. 4:10 NLT)

As he did in the life of Jabez, God wants to enlarge our territory so our Christian influence can be expanded. He wants to bring wisdom and provision and health and witty inventions to the people of God—not so we can have a Lexus in the three-car garage of our brick mansion with the built-in pool and sound system—but so we can make him known to fallen man and cooperate with the Holy Spirit to see the kingdom of God established in the world.

Remember, money is not in itself evil. The Bible says "*the love of money* is the root of all kinds of evil" (1 Tim. 6:10 NLT, emphasis added). Money is a necessary part of living and a proper understanding of it is needed to live a life that is meaningful and productive. In the movie *It's a Wonderful Life*, Clarence the angel tells George Bailey they don't use money in heaven. A despondent George replies, "Well it comes in handy down here, Bub!"

There is an old saying, "money makes the world go round." In this world, money and resources are necessary to get things done, both secular and sacred. I've been in full-time vocational ministry in various capacities throughout my adult life. In that time, I've learned an important lesson—people and resources and equipment and money are required to accomplish things for God. Some people may be shocked at that statement, but there is no denying its truth.

It takes money to run any organization—from your family to your local church, to Wal-Mart, to the Billy Graham Evangelistic Association. This concept is as true in the church and in ministries as it is in the world.

Years ago, I learned an important lesson while watching *Larry King Live*. On one evening, Oral and Evelyn Roberts were guests on the program. Larry King brought up the subject of money and the concerns raised by some who felt Oral Roberts had spent too much time focused on fund-raising. Oral pointed out it takes money to operate a college and a television ministry. He explained a ministry is no different than a secular business that charges fees for a service, or a television network that runs commercials in the middle of their programs.

After several moments of conversation, Larry King turned to the camera and announced, "We have to take a commercial break, and we will be right back ..."

Oral Roberts interrupted him and said, "You mean you are going to take an offering."

King smiled, pointed his finger at Roberts, and declared, "Touché."

We all need God's provision to be effective in reaching out to people with the gospel. That doesn't only mean financial provision. Every person and ministry also requires God's provision of wisdom, creativity, talented and faithful people, proper facilities, technology, equipment, raw materials, transportation, communication—and on and on and on.

The problems we face in the twenty-first century are truly staggering. Now, more than ever, the world needs strong Christians who are full of faith. We need believers who know how to receive grace and favor from God to help find solutions and answers to these dilemmas. These problems require Christians who know their God, who stand firm, and who will act in his name (Dan. 11:32).

The Peter, Paul, and Mary principle is all about learning how to hear God's voice, recognizing his direction, and then seeing his will fulfilled by faith and honest to goodness hard work.

This book is an examination of three critical moments and the vital responses in faith that made all the difference—in the lives of these three people, in the history of the church, and in the history of the world. We will thoroughly dissect this principle to help us discover the power that comes by being a person of faith. The Peter, Paul, and Mary principle is a gift from our loving heavenly Father to help us unlock the storehouse of heaven, so we can unravel mysteries, provide answers, and share God's blessings to meet the needs of his creation. It is quite an adventure—and I believe this principle will truly change your life.

—CHAPTER TWO—
PETER: AN UNLIKELY HERO OF FAITH

He was a successful businessman—a tradesman, heartily plying his craft with a small fleet of fishing boats he shared with his brother and associates. He knew the sea, his boats, his friends, his family—and as a God-fearing Jewish man, he knew his religion.

But religion came second to business for this man called Simon—whose name would later be changed by Jesus to Peter. And besides, didn't the religious leaders even fall short of the mark? He figured the principles of Judaism were an important part of life, but not the most important. Next to his love for God, providing a living for his family was most important.

Peter was well-respected among his peers. He was tough. He was wise to the ways of the world. He was no nonsense. He called things the way he saw them—no frills, no pretense, no foolishness. He was the kind of man who would fish all night to bring in a catch to make sure the needs of his family were met.

So, when this young religious teacher arrived in his hometown of Capernaum on the banks of the Sea of Galilee, Peter paid little attention to the excited chatter. That changed one day when Jesus decided to teach the multitudes on the shore.

Peter, his brother Andrew, and their friends James and John had had another difficult, exhausting night. Even with all the years of experience and the tricks of the trade, sometimes we come up empty-handed. After fishing all night with no success, Peter and his colleagues were tired and frustrated. The crowd pressing around them as they cleaned their nets grated on Peter's nerves. The nets needed to be stowed, and he wanted to hurry home to get a few hours of sleep before trying again later that day.

Suddenly, Jesus called to him. "Simon, I'm going to jump into your boat. Push me out a little way so the crowd can hear me better."

"Oh great," Peter might have thought, "I'm going to have to wait until he's done preaching before I can go home." Now boiling with frustration, Peter had little choice. The entire town had gathered to hear this rabbi. How would he look to his friends and customers if he refused? Reluctantly, he invited the rabbi aboard and pushed out into deeper water.

Jesus stood in the small craft and began teaching the crowd, his voice amplified on the water. Peter tried to ignore him as he continued tidying up the nets, but even through his frustration, the words spoken by this young teacher captured his attention. This was not pretentious oratory, full of the religious platitudes he heard from other teachers of the law. The teaching of Jesus was simple, straight to the point, and remarkably practical.

Simon continued working on the nets, but the rabbi had his ear. Jesus had grabbed Peter's attention, now he would capture his heart.

After he finished his sermon, Jesus called to Simon, "Take your boat out into the deeper water and let down your nets for a catch."

Peter had just finished stowing his neatly folded nets. The impromptu religious service was over. The boat was tidy. It was time to go home. Who did this teacher think he was talking to anyway? The fish weren't cooperating.

Standing chest-deep in the water next to the boat, Simon paused for a moment to assess the situation. He didn't want to be rude. After all, this was an impressive teacher of the law.

Looking up at Jesus he responded with a slight laugh. "Master, we have fished all night and caught nothing …"

He paused, waiting for Jesus to respond. Surely the teacher would yield to the wisdom of a seasoned fisherman. Jesus didn't bat an eye. He simply smiled and waited for Peter to enter the world of wonder that lay before him.

The seafarer looked around for support from his partners, but their raised eyebrows and puzzled expressions provided no means of escape. The whole town stood on the shoreline waiting for his response. Again, he laughed and turned his face toward Jesus. Slowly the words slipped passed his lips, "… but at your word, we'll let down our nets." Though exhausted, the small band smiled as they climbed into the boats and pushed out to sea, destined to begin an adventure of faith that would take them beyond their wildest dreams.

Simon Peter knew exactly where he wanted to go—just out far enough to be in the deep water, but not so far that they couldn't get back to shore quickly when they proved to Jesus who knew more about fishing.

The young rabbi sat silently in the bow of the vessel. A slight smile raised the corners of his mouth as he watched the men methodically carrying out their assignments. Peter was particularly gruff as he barked out orders. He was used to being in charge, and he didn't like being led where he didn't want to go, especially when he was tired. "Come on, John, pay attention. Keep the lines tight," he snarled at the youngest of the group.

At the count of three, they heaved the nets into the turquoise-colored water. Immediately the nets churned with activity. Across the surface of the sea, silver-bellied fish slithered over each other in a frenzied dance. Instinct took over, and Peter hollered, "Bring them in! Together, pull!" The men snapped into action, the muscles in their arms and legs straining as they pulled hundreds of glimmering fish into the boats. The weight of the catch was so massive the nets themselves began to tear.

Jesus joined in the laughter as he watched the men fill both vessels so full of fish they began to sink dangerously close to the water line. "Bail some of the catch, quickly," Peter hollered to his mates.

As the fish writhed and hopped in the bottom of the boat, Jesus stood to grab the mainsail. Suddenly, the reality of the situation struck Peter, and he shuddered. This was certainly not a normal catch, and the person now standing above him, his long hair whipping in the Galilean wind, was no ordinary man. Peter stopped to look up at Jesus. He felt as if the rabbi was looking right through him. He felt almost naked before him, like Jesus was reading his thoughts and seeing everything he had ever done.

Losing all strength, he fell to his knees among the fish at Jesus's feet. Unable to meet his gaze, Peter implored in a quivering voice, "Depart from me, Lord, for I am a sinful man."

The others stopped their activity to watch the drama unfold. With gentleness and compassion, Jesus leaned over and placed his hand on the back of Peter's neck. Trembling, the fisherman looked up through tears as Jesus declared, "Don't be afraid. From now on, you will be a fisher of men."

Peter couldn't comprehend what the rabbi meant by this, but he did know his life would never be the same.

When Jesus gave Peter the command to follow him, the fisherman did so without hesitation. Obeying was the beginning of an odyssey with Christ that would challenge and perplex him—that would take him from the dizzying heights of transfiguration and miraculous power to the grinding depths of betrayal and bewilderment.

And along the way, Jesus would provide one opportunity after another for this outspoken, natural born leader to be tested, and tried, and sifted like wheat. But in the end, Jesus would establish Peter as an apostle of faith. And on the day of Pentecost, by the power of the Holy Spirit, Peter would shake himself loose from the coils of his ordinary life and enter an extraordinary existence that would rock the ancient world to its foundations.

Later, when the Jewish religious leaders saw the boldness of Peter and perceived he was an uneducated fisherman, they marveled and realized he had been with Jesus (Acts 4:13).

Peter's Moment of Faith

In obedience to the call of Christ, Peter left his nets behind and followed Jesus as one of the twelve apostles. Later, one of the greatest tests of Peter's faith came amid the tragic circumstance surrounding the beheading of John the Baptist by the evil King Herod. When Jesus heard the news of John's death, he withdrew from the multitude—needing to be alone with his Father (Matthew 14).

Besides being his natural cousin, John the Baptist was, spiritually speaking, the closest person to Jesus on earth. And now he was gone—brutally butchered by a tyrannical king.

After receiving the news, Jesus asked his disciples to take him by boat to a solitary place. But by now he had grown so popular he couldn't go anywhere without a multitude of people flocking to see him—even in the most remote locations.

When they landed on the far shore, the crowd was there waiting for them. Though Jesus was exhausted and grieving, he was moved with compassion by the needs of the people. Moving through the crowd he reached out and healed all those who were sick. Later he fed them all—more than five thousand—with only five loaves and two fish.

When they had finished eating, Jesus sent the multitude away and told his disciples to go before him to the other side of the sea. After everyone had gone, Jesus went up on the mountain by himself to spend time with his Father in prayer.

Rowing to the middle of the sea, the disciples soon found themselves in the middle of a howling storm. The tempest had arisen rapidly, without warning, and the disciples were soon frightened for their lives. Frantically they worked to keep the small wooden vessel afloat, desperately rowing for shore and bailing water.

Suddenly, across the surface of the water, a shadowy figure appeared from out of the darkness. The Old Testament is filled with examples from the spiritual realm, so the disciples wondered what this image could be—perhaps an angel, or worse, a ghost. Perhaps they were about to sink beneath the waves, and this was the angel of death preparing to gather their souls.

But the figure wasn't a ghost. It was Jesus, once again spinning a life experience to test their faith and drive home a lesson they would never forget.

"It's me," Jesus cried over the howling wind. "Don't be afraid."

This is the point where the Peter, Paul, and Mary principle begins to unfold. Let's dissect the concept as we see it revealed in this event.

THE PETER, PAUL, AND MARY PRINCIPLE EXPLAINED

I've highlighted the elements of the principle from Matthew's account (Matthew 14:25–29 NASB):

In the fourth watch of the night (A) He came to them, walking on the sea. (B) When the disciples saw Him walking on the sea, they were terrified, and said, "It is a ghost!" And they cried out in fear. (C) But immediately Jesus spoke to them, saying, "Take courage, it is I; do not be afraid." (D) Peter said to him, "Lord, if it is You, command me to come to You on the water." (E) And He said, "Come." (F & G) And Peter got out of the boat, (H) and walked on the water and came toward Jesus.

Now, let's examine the principle piece by piece.

A. **God initiates the communication. (Matthew 14:25)**

First, we must recognize in any encounter with heaven, God is who initiates the communication. We may think we've set out on our search for truth, but the reality is God had been working in our lives from the moment we were conceived, the Holy Spirit drawing us to a relationship with him through Jesus Christ.

God is sovereign, which means he rules in the affairs of men—whether we recognize his sovereignty or not. Mankind, in its fallen state, doesn't usually pursue communication with God unless there is a perception something can be gained from that communication—or if we need God to get us out of a scrape. God, on the other hand, epitomizes the fullness of love (1 John 4:8)—and love communicates.

Therefore, God always initiates communication with man. Paul shows how God has been at work well before we even considered seeking him.

> But God demonstrates His own love toward us, in that while we were still sinners, Christ died for us. (Romans. 5:8 NASB)

In the garden of Eden, when Adam and Eve disobeyed God by eating the forbidden fruit, they hid themselves in shame. Yet despite their failure, God came looking for them. Genesis tells us God's habit was to communicate with Adam and Eve in the cool of the day (Gen. 3:8). Though the man and woman tried to cover their sin, God sought them out and communicated with them from a heart of love.

God remains the same today.

In the case of Peter, Jesus initiated the communication by walking out to the disciples on the water.

> B. **When God invades our world, we often don't know it is him, and this fills us with anxiety. (Matthew 14:26)**

When the disciples see Jesus, they are filled with fear and don't know who is coming to them on the water. Most people have the same feeling when they first have an encounter with God.

> C. **God always comes to us in peace. (Matthew 14:27)**

The next thing we observe from this passage is God always comes to us in peace, dispelling all fear. To comfort his disciples, Jesus said, "It is I. Do not be afraid."

Peace is like a God detector. When we are seeking direction for our lives, the peace of God is what helps us to decide between the many options we face.

God will always come to us in peace. Now, someone may not initially sense that peace, especially if they have never had an encounter with God. Like the disciples, they may be afraid, worried the encounter may be harmful. But as we see in this passage of Scripture, Jesus assures them it is he, and with this assurance comes the peace of God. He will do the same for you and me.

> D. **We wonder, 'Is it really God?' (Matthew 14:28)**

The next thing we notice is Peter trying to determine if what he is seeing and hearing is really from God.

> And Peter answered him and said, "Lord, **if it is You**, command me to come to you on the water." (Matthew 14:28, italics and emphasis added)

We often do the same thing when God is trying to get our attention. "Is that really you, God? How do I know it's not just my imagination? Perhaps it's only some religious idea?"

If you are a Christian, do you remember what you experienced when God first got your attention? You knew someone was trying to reach you, but who was it? "Is it a wandering spirit?" "Is it Allah?" "Is it Krishna or another Hindu god?" "Could it be the devil?"

The things of God were foreign to you. You may have felt worldly things made sense, and the ways of God were odd, unusual, or even evil—like Neo's experience in the movie *The Matrix*. You may have questioned if the things you were hearing from other Christians were really of God or just some manmade religious system of dos and don'ts.

At first, the disciples thought this being on the water was a ghost—surely not a being sent from God—and certainly not the Son of God. But when Peter heard those gentle words amid the howling storm, "It is I; do not be afraid," he likely remembered that earlier encounter when Jesus filled his boat with fish and his heart with hope. "This just might be God," he may have thought, and he took a chance that changed his entire outlook on life.

"Lord, if it is you..." he blurted out.

Notice he began his question with the assumption the figure was in fact the Lord. It's as if God has built into each one of us a gyroscope or a homing device that leads us to him. Most humankind is seeking after God, even though often for selfish reasons. We build churches, temples, cathedrals, synagogues, mosques, and altars to God. If there is some aberration or prophet claiming to be from

God, thousands flock to see. This fact should give us a great deal of comfort. The Bible promises that if we seek God, we will find him, if we seek with all our heart (Jeremiah 29:13).

The born-again believer has the assurance we will find the truth and know God's leading. "My sheep hear My voice," Jesus promises. "And when he has brought out his own, he goes before them, and the sheep follow him, for they know his voice. A stranger they will not follow, but will flee from him, for they do not know the voice of strangers" (John 10:4–5).

Throughout the Scriptures we have God's promise he will show us the way. "Call to Me and I will answer you, and I will tell you great and mighty things, which you do not know" (Jeremiah 33:3 NASB).

Like you and me, Peter needed assurance God was really talking to him. "Lord, if it is you, bid me come to you on the water." Coming from the mouth of an experienced fisherman, this sounds like a ridiculous statement. Peter knew the danger of being out on the water in a storm. I don't think this was his own thought he was speaking. I believe the Holy Spirit planted the thought in Peter's mind, and since he had little control over his tongue at that time, I think the words just spilled out of his mouth.

God is not limited by the grandness of our request. In fact, I believe God wants us to ask big, for his kingdom's sake, so the only way we can succeed is if God intervenes to answer our prayer. Peter asked big—and Jesus responded big. "Come!" He declares. With one word the ball is back in Peter's court.

E. **God will always call us to a higher level in him.**

In a sense, Jesus called Peter's bluff, calling him to a higher level of faith. In *The Last Battle*, the final book of the Chronicles of Narnia, C. S. Lewis repeats the phrase, "further up, and further in." This is a key part of our walk with God. Scripture speaks of us going from "strength to strength."

> They will continue to grow stronger, and each of them will appear before God in Jerusalem. (Psalm 84:7 NLT)

The Bible tells us that our victory comes through our faith.

> For every child of God defeats this evil world, and we achieve this victory through our faith. (1 John 5:4 NLT)

Scripture expounds on this upward call of God:

> The path of the righteous is like the light of dawn, which shines **brighter and brighter** until full day. (Proverbs 4:18, italics and emphasis added)

F. **We recognize the communication is from God, and we have to make a decision to trust him.**

While every step in this process is important, the decision stage is especially critical. Up to this point in Peter's encounter, everything in the principle occurs in the realm of the spirit and soul, which is our connection to God (spirit), and our own mind, will, and emotions (soul). But nothing changes in this world as long as the process remains spirit/soul. Only when God's plan is brought into the natural realm by faith and corresponding action does change occur.

Taking the process from spirit/soul to natural realm first requires *a decision on our part.*

Billy Graham preached the gospel to people all over the world in his lifetime, and in every message, he shared the message of salvation (spirit/soul), but then, he led his listeners to the inevitable point of decision. Thousands of times, in hundreds of countries, to millions of people he declared, "Now is the time of decision. You can come to Christ just as you are."

Peter was also faced with a decision. Jesus had him pinned in a corner. Peter would have to fish or cut bait, figuratively speaking. Would he obey the call of God in faith despite the stormy sea? Or would he shrink back in fear and doubt—even though he knew he had heard the word of the Lord.

This is where the Peter, Paul, and Mary principle moves beyond the spiritual realm into the natural dimension. Remember the critical admonition of the apostle James we mentioned in chapter one:

> Faith by itself, if it does not have works, is dead. (James 2:17)

Because man is made from the dust of the ground, and he has been given delegated authority on this earth, there is always a natural dimension in our interaction with God. In the garden of Eden, God delegated authority to humans on the earth, and the earth is a physical place with natural laws. Therefore, all we receive from God must go from the spiritual to the natural realm.

Some have said only someone in an "earth suit" has this delegated authority from God. That is why humankind is in charge on this planet. God created men and women man as a spirit beings, but he placed our spirits within an earthly vessel—or as the apostle Paul put it, "an earthly tent" (2 Corinthians 5:1). Before Christ was revealed, God related to humans in the spirit. But the apostle John tells us the Father sent Jesus to earth as a man.

> And the Word became flesh and dwelt among us, and we have seen his glory, the glory as the only Son, full of grace and truth. (John 1:14)

It's interesting to note the word "dwelt" in this passage is the same word as tabernacle or tent. Jesus took on the same tent that we have—the same "earth suit." He became one of us. This is a vital part of our redemption, and the significance can be traced back before the fall of man in the Garden when God promised a redeemer to mankind.

When it was time for a decision, Peter chose faith.

> G. **Once we've responded to God's call, we must take corresponding action to seal the promise.**

Once Peter decided to act in faith, he lifted his foot over the side of that small wooden boat. If he hadn't acted on his decision, things would have remained in the spirit/soul realm, and nothing would have changed. But Peter's action pulled the scenario from the spiritual into the natural world. Change was now inevitable.

> H. **Our faith and corresponding action, mixed with the Word of God and his grace, brings the promise of heaven into fruition, enabling us to receive from God.**

This is the final, wondrous part of the Peter, Paul, and Mary principle. The instant that Simon Peter's foot touched that churning water, God's wondrous grace joined with Peter's faith and corresponding action, and the miracle of a man walking with God on the water occurred.

This is the Peter, Paul, and Mary principle—and the way you and I receive anything from God. Understanding this concept is an important key that can open the door to the victorious Christian life.

Peter received his miracle as a result of God's love. To the amazement of the other disciples, he started walking toward Jesus on the water. But the miracle was short-lived. When the fisherman saw the large waves, he allowed fear to creep back into his heart. When Peter abandoned faith and began to fear, he immediately started to sink.

This is an important postscript to the Peter, Paul, and Mary principle—fear is a faith killer. Eliminate faith and we eliminate our miracle.

Peter knew the source of his salvation, and even in his fear he cried out, "Lord, save me!" In an act of gentle compassion, Jesus reached out and pulled Peter to the surface. Together they climbed back into the boat, and the wind ceased. Immediately, the disciples dropped to their knees and worshipped Christ.

In the months to come, the faith of these disciples would be greatly tested as Jesus went to the cross in Jerusalem. Peter would succumb to fear and temptation again and again—even denying Jesus three times on the night of his betrayal. But again and again and again, Jesus would forgive Peter and restore him with love and grace.

In the end, Peter would rise as the leader God had intended him to be. And on the day of Pentecost, he would be God's spokesman, leading three thousand to salvation in one day.

As Obi-Wan Kenobi said to Luke in *Star Wars: A New Hope*[1]: "You must learn the ways of the force, if you're to come with me to Alderaan." You see, Star Wars is yet another parable of the celestial battle between good and evil. But the war for heaven and earth as described in the Bible is no mere myth. Whether we understand or not, we're a part of a pitched spiritual battle between the forces of good and the minions of evil. Like Luke Skywalker, we must learn the ways of the Holy Spirit if we're to be effective in the fight. The Peter, Paul, and Mary principle is one of the most important tools for the child of God because it unleashes a most powerful spiritual weapon—faith.

—CHAPTER THREE—
PAUL: A DETOUR ON THE ROAD OF FAITH

You couldn't find a man who was more different from Peter than the Pharisee, Saul of Tarsus—who later became the apostle Paul. Where Peter was gruff, uneducated, and backward, Paul was refined, a Pharisee of Pharisees, and as religious and sophisticated as a Jerusalem Jew could be in the first century.

But like Peter, Paul was not initially interested in becoming a follower of Christ. To the contrary, this pious man was bent on the destruction of the Jewish believers in Jesus.

To understand Saul of Tarsus, it's important we place him into historical context. Only a few years had passed from the crucifixion and resurrection of Jesus when a self-righteous religious zealot assisted in the infamous stoning murder of one of Christianity's earliest messengers, a godly man named Stephen.

> Then they cast him [Stephen] out of the city and stoned him. And the witnesses laid down their garments at the feet of a young man named Saul. And as they were stoning Stephen, he called out God, "Lord Jesus, receive my spirit." Falling to his knees he cried out with a loud

voice, "Lord, do not hold this sin against them." And when he had said this, he fell asleep. (Acts. 7:58–60)

Luke punctuates Saul's involvement in this brutal murder: "Now Saul was consenting to his death."

"The best and the brightest." It was a phrase used by some journalists to describe the administration of President John F. Kennedy. The same words could have been used to describe Saul of Tarsus—a child of the best upbringing; a student of the vaunted teacher, Gamaliel; a Roman citizen; trained in the best Jewish schools; groomed to become one of the elite religious leaders of first century Israel.

But even before that fateful day when young Saul the Pharisee gloated over the heinous death of the innocent disciple Stephen, the Spirit of Jesus Christ had been pricking his heart. God had designs for this bright young man, and in his sovereignty, he was prepared to knock Saul off his high horse.

There can be little doubt Saul was familiar with the Galilean man known as Jesus. Though he may have been consumed by his study of the Torah and Talmud—the Jewish holy books—under his mentor, the wise and respected Gamaliel, there was surely talk of this backwoods preacher and the stir he was making throughout occupied Israel. Though continuous reports circulated of so-called messiahs emerging from every corner of the land, Saul and his colleagues undoubtedly debated the authenticity of the reports being made of Jesus and his miracles.

Who knows? Perhaps Saul was one of the unnamed lawyers or scribes who confronted Jesus with questions in the gospel accounts? Saul may have gathered with the other Pharisees and religious leaders at the river Jordan when John the Baptist declared, "Behold, the Lamb of God who takes away the sin of the world." Was he outraged to learn Jesus had cleared the moneychangers and vendors of religious trinkets from the temple while snapping a whip?

It is even conceivable Saul was one of the pious Pharisees trying to console a weeping Mary and Martha at the death of their brother Lazarus. Whether he was physically present when Jesus raised the three-day-dead Lazarus from his rotting rest, it is likely that Saul—along with most of Jerusalem—heard about and pondered this indisputable miracle. The Pharisees at the gravesite knew that Lazarus was stone-cold, stinking dead. In their religious manner, as was the custom, they were trying to console his sisters. Suddenly, Jesus appeared on the scene, two days late. When Jesus cried out, "Come forth," these religious leaders witnessed the real "dead man walking."

Word of these events flashed through Jerusalem like a bolt of lightning, shaking the Sanhedrin to their very core. This shocking development created such a sensation among the people the panicked religious leaders immediately ramped up their efforts to arrest and execute this backwater mystic before he whipped the masses into a frenzy. They feared an uncontrolled mob could bring down the wrath of Rome.

Though the Bible doesn't reveal it, Saul could have attended the infamous midnight trial of Jesus before the Sanhedrin—an illegal trial so corrupt, any fair-minded lawyer would have blushed. Perhaps Saul was outside in the courtyard of Caiaphas warming himself next to the fire. Maybe he heard the servant girl accusing a gruff-looking Galilean of being a follower of this Jesus. He may have been amused at the unrefined way this fisherman cursed and raved the third time he was accused.

Though Saul approved of the barbarous stoning of Stephen, it's entirely possible his heart was pricked when he heard this heroic servant of God utter words of forgiveness that can only come from the Spirit of Christ, "Lord, do not charge them with this sin."

We don't know how long the Lord was at work in the heart of Saul, but we know the Holy Spirit was goading him, and Saul was kicking back.

He was kicking back hard—primarily against the disciples of Jesus Christ. The Bible tells us after the death of Stephen, Saul fanatically set out to destroy this new sect. Along with other radical Pharisees, Saul launched a holy war against the early church. The persecution spread from Jerusalem, scattering the believers throughout the regions of Judea and Samaria.

Saul used his influence as one of the leading students of Gamaliel to obtain permission from the high priest to harass and silence these believers in Jesus. Of course, the high priest and the rulers of the Sanhedrin were more than happy to grant Saul these powers. I wonder what the Romans thought of Saul's behavior. Along with an armed band of thugs, Saul began tormenting, threatening, then actually beating and arresting the disciples. He made havoc among the early disciples, entering homes, dragging off men and women, sending many to prison—even putting some to death. Saul grew increasingly menacing and soon all of Jerusalem, Judea, and the surrounding region knew of his witch hunt.

He gained the notoriety and favor of men. he had craved since his youth. He knew this was only the beginning. If he was going to rise to the level of prestige and power he believed was his destiny, he would have to prove himself worthy. This was his chance.

Word came to the high priest that these followers of Jesus had spread beyond Samaria and into Syria (Acts 9). Saul requested permission to go to Damascus to extend his expedition of terror. With great delight, the high priest granted him letters to take to the synagogues of Damascus so if they found any who were of "the Way"—an early name for the church—whether men or women, Saul would be empowered to bring them bound to Jerusalem.

Yes, this journey to Damascus would be a crowning achievement in an already stellar religious career.

As he and his colleagues came near Damascus, suddenly Saul and his companions were flooded with the most glorious light imaginable. It was like being deluged in liquid sunlight. It pierced their skin and flooded into the depths of their very souls. Saul lost all control of his faculties. Like a dead man he fell to the dusty road. Coming to his senses, he rose from the ground and looked in every direction, but all around him was bright luminescence.

To his astonishment, a voice emanated from within the light. Saul recognized the light radiated from a presence—from a person. The sound of the voice was terrifying and soothing at the same time—like the way a lion cub feels at the sound of its father's roar. Saul felt fear, security, and awe all at the same time. "Saul, Saul," the majestic voice declared. "Why are you persecuting me? It is hard for you to kick against the goads."

"Who could this be?" Saul wondered. Was this an angel? Or worse, could it be a messenger from Satan, trying to distract him from his holy quest? No, if it were the devil, he wouldn't feel this warmth—a presence he had felt before, but only on a few precious occasions. He could see nothing but overwhelming light. Raising his hand to shield his eyes, in humility he inquired, "Who are you, Lord?"

"I am Jesus, whom you are persecuting."

No. It couldn't be. It couldn't be Jesus, the carpenter from Nazareth, the backwoods preacher, the so-called messiah who was put to death by Pontius Pilate so recently. If this was Jesus, then nearly every great leader in Israel was wrong ... so very, very wrong. How could they have misjudged him? Unless ... unless those confusing passages of Scripture concerning a suffering savior could, somehow speak of the Messiah?

Saul began to tremble.

How could he be so wrong? But then he remembered watching the life ebbing from Stephen, and hearing those haunting words, "Lord, do not charge them with this sin ..." and, "Lord Jesus, receive my spirit."

Was this the same Jesus Stephen saw as he peered into heaven? Was he the one who gave strength and peace to so many of Saul's victims? Saul began shaking uncontrollably. No longer able to bear the intensity of the light, he closed his eyes as tightly as he could.

"It must be true," he thought. "This must be the One—the glorious Messiah, promised from ages past." Saul slowly lifted his head and asked, "Lord, what do you want me to do?"

Jesus replied, "Arise and go into the city, and you will be told what you must do."

Despite the risk to his life from his fellow Pharisees, Saul obeyed, and his life was radically changed. In time, he so identified with the radical call God gave to him to reach the gentiles, he changed his name from the Jewish "Saul," to the gentile "Paul"—the name I use in the Peter, Paul, and Mary principle?

Paul and the Principle

Let's compare this event on the road to Damascus with the different points of the Peter, Paul, and Mary principle:

A. First, it is God who initiates the communication on the road to Damascus. Saul wasn't looking to have a conversation with Jesus. He was going about his merry old murderous business. He wasn't seeking God at that moment, though in his religious mind he may have thought he was. But Jesus was seeking him, and he had been for some time.

As he had with Moses in the Old Testament, God prepared Saul for a ministry beyond his wildest imagination. Moses was also trained in the best schools. And just as God confronted Moses and redirected his life when he least expected it, revealing himself in the burning bush, God now confronted Saul when he least expected him, revealing himself amid a great light.

- B. In fear, Saul questioned whether it was God. "Who are you, Lord?" It's interesting both Peter and Paul address the being before them by using the term "Lord"—a title that indicates superiority, authority, and greatness.

- C. In this scenario, we don't hear Jesus bring peace through his words, as we do in the encounters with Peter and Mary, but we can infer Saul had enough peace to obey Jesus's command to go into Damascus and wait for further instructions.

- D. Jesus reveals himself to Saul and asks him why he is struggling against the goads. As we have observed, this was not the first time the Holy Spirit confronted Saul with the reality of Jesus as the Christ. The Spirit of God was goading him, and Saul was kicking against the pricks. Saul is clearly questioning who it is behind this majestic voice and brilliant light.

- E. Jesus has revealed himself to this young Pharisee for a purpose. What could it be? Saul asks the question. "Lord, what do you want me to do?" Jesus calls Saul to a higher level with his command: "Go into the city and you will be told what to do."

F. Now the ball is back in Saul's court. It's decision time. Just as quickly as Jesus appeared, he disappeared, leaving Saul and his comrades befuddled and confused. Saul rose to his feet and realized he couldn't see. How would he respond to the heavenly vision and to his current lack of sight?

He could have explained it all away as a fainting spell or some sort of hallucination. Perhaps the Middle Eastern heat overtook him, causing him to faint and fall to the ground. Maybe he hit his head when he struck the ground, causing the loss of sight. And while he was unconscious, he fell into a dreamlike state, experiencing a hallucination straight from the devil himself.

But no hallucination ever felt so peaceful. No dream ever gave the sense of complete security as he felt on that dusty road outside Damascus.

Yes, Saul had a decision to make. Would he ignore the divine appointment Jesus set, living out his life as the greatest blind Pharisee of the age? Or would he risk his reputation, and possibly his life, to obey the words of Jesus?

And what about his buddies? How would the religious henchmen react to this scenario? They had set out from Jerusalem intent on harassing and imprisoning the followers of Jesus. What would they do if their leader himself suddenly became a follower of Christ? Like Saul they had heard the regal voice, but they had seen nothing. Saul knew obeying Jesus could immediately cost him his life at the hands of his own posse.

Saul made his decision. He would obey the directions of the Lord.

G. Once a decision is made, there must be corresponding action. Saul had to get up from where he was and make his way into Damascus. He picked himself up from the ground and announced his destination.

Remarkably, his friends led him by the hand the rest of the way into the city. For the next three days, Saul sat in blindness, pondering the dumbfounding experience with Jesus on the Damascus road. During that time, he neither ate nor drank as he waited for further instructions from the Lord.

Saul spent those three days in intense prayer. The Bible tells us that at some point he had another vision. This time, he saw a man named Ananias coming in and placing his hand on him in prayer so that he would once again be able to see.

This same Ananias had his own test of faith. He, too, received a vision from the Lord. Jesus said to him, "Arise, and go to the street called Straight, and inquire in the house of Judas for one called Saul of Tarsus, for behold he is praying."

Ananias must have wondered if Jesus meant "praying" or "preying." In a tone of significant caution, he responded, "Lord, I have heard from many about this man, how much evil he has done to your saints in Jerusalem. And here he has the authority from the chief priests to bind all who call on your name" (Acts 9:13). Saul's fame had preceded him.

"But the Lord said to him, 'Go, for he is a chosen instrument of mine to carry my name before Gentiles and kings and the children of Israel. For I will show him how much he must suffer for the sake of my name'" (Acts 9:15–16).

And so, this courageous disciple obeyed the instructions of the Lord and sought out Saul in the house of Judas.

H. Saul and Ananias both acted on the instructions given to them, giving feet to their faith. Ananias entered the house of Judas and laid his hands on Saul saying, "Brother Saul, the Lord Jesus, who appeared to you on the road as you came, has sent me that you may receive your sight and be filled with the Holy Spirit." With this action on the word of the Lord, God's grace came on the scene and immediately there fell from Saul's eyes something like scales. He received his sight at once. Saul sealed the deal when he arose to be baptized.

The Peter, Paul, and Mary principle was clearly evidenced in the dramatic events of Saul's conversion—an experience that would be the beginning of the transformation of a pious Pharisee named Saul into a humble disciple of Jesus Christ, whose name was changed to Paul.

A. God initiated the communication.

B. We hear the voice and are filled with fear, confusion, and anxiety.

C. God brings his peace.

D. We wonder if it is God communicating.

E. God always calls us to a higher level.

F. People recognize the communication is from God and must decide whether to act on God's instruction.

G. Once they've decided, they must act accordingly, taking the experience from the spiritual into the natural realm.

H. In faith, the action is taken, based on the instruction of the Lord. At that moment, the grace of God comes on the scene, mixing with the Word of God, the faith, and the action—in this case bringing about the miracle of the restoration of Saul's sight, and his baptism into the ministry of a disciple of Jesus Christ.

Saul's decision to follow Christ made him a part of the family of God that included an ex-crusty old fisherman, who was now fishing for men. The family also included a wise woman of God who was once a young virgin in the town of Nazareth. She was a descendent of King David, though her modest dwelling and humble existence would not have revealed that family ancestry. This fair young maiden's heart had been enraptured by the dealings of Almighty God—a woman of faith that the world would come to know as Mary.

—CHAPTER FOUR—
MARY: A SHINING EXAMPLE OF FAITH

Mark Lowery captured the world's imagination when he penned the tender, yet haunting, words in "Mary Did You Know" that so aptly describe the earthly mother of Jesus—the vessel through which the incarnate Son of God would be brought into this world.

One must wonder if this teenaged girl from the tiny village of Nazareth in Galilee truly comprehended what God was asking of her. Her response of faith to God's request is why she is a part of the Peter, Paul, and Mary principle.

Many biblical scholars believe Mary was in her mid-teens when God's messenger angel appeared to her. She was entering into an exciting and somewhat anxious time in her life. In this era of arranged marriages, she had been betrothed, or promised, to a local carpenter by the name of Joseph. All the wonderful experiences of the grown-up world lay before her as she anticipated marriage and children. We don't know how long before the wedding date Gabriel spoke to Mary, but we do know his appearance initially caused great fear in the heart of this young Jewish girl.

"Greetings, favored woman!" Gabriel began, "The Lord is with you!" (Luke 1:28 NLT)

The appearance of this mighty angel frightened Mary, as it would most likely terrify you and me. But the angel of God immediately put her heart at ease, saying, "Don't be afraid, Mary, for you have found favor with God!" (Luke 1:30 NLT) I imagine this brought a measure of peace to the young girl, but what the angel said next probably sent her into another tailspin.

"You will conceive and give birth to a son, and you will name him Jesus. He will be very great and will be called the Son of the Most High. The Lord God will give him the throne of his ancestor David. And he will reign over Israel forever; his Kingdom will never end!" (vv. 31–33 NLT)

Can you imagine how overwhelming this encounter must have been for Mary? First, to be confronted by an angelic being the likes of Gabriel, one of the archangels no less; to be told that you have been singled out, not only from all the young maidens outside Israel, but also from all the women of God's chosen people; and then to be told your child would occupy the throne of King David—the greatest desire of every mother for her child in Israel.

"Why me?" she must have wondered. "Why here? Why now?"

The most pressing question was the one she let slip from her mouth, "But how can this happen? I am a virgin." (v. 34 NLT) Yes, she was betrothed to Joseph, but in ancient Israel the betrothal was an engagement period of an unspecified length of time. Joseph and Mary had not consummated their marriage.

This question did not indicate a lack of faith on Mary's part. It was simply a technical issue to her. The angel of the Lord addressed her question with a straightforward answer.

"The Holy Spirit will come upon you, and the power of the Most High will overshadow you. So the baby to be born will be holy, and he will be called the Son of God." (v. 35 NLT)

To demonstrate God's ability to do that which seems impossible to man, the angel offered a sign to Mary. "What's more, your relative Elizabeth has become pregnant in her old age! People used to say she was barren, but she has conceived a son and is now in her sixth month. For the word of God will never fail." (vv. 36–37 NLT).

Another version renders the last sentence: "For with God nothing will be impossible."

One wonders how long Mary pondered these things in her heart before responding to the angel. She knew, like all first century Jewish women did, that the consequences for being found pregnant outside of marriage could have meant death. Other young women had been stoned in the street for such a violation of Jewish law. Mary must have wondered how a pregnancy would affect her family. Would they receive the scorn of the community? Would they be outcasts because of her?

And what of Joseph, her betrothed? He was a good man—a kind man. Her father had been so wise to have arranged a marriage with such a godly gentleman. Wouldn't he be disgraced as well?

How would Mary tell Joseph? It would seem to be a story beyond belief. Did Mary expect he would accept her explanation of a glorious angel appearing from nowhere and promising the Holy Spirit would cause her to become pregnant?

Wouldn't he think she was out of her mind?

And what of the proposal itself? To carry the Son of God in her womb? It must have been a mind-numbing proposition. What would such a child be like? How would he behave? How could she and Joseph teach God?

Would he know he was God from the start? If not, how old would he be before he realized who he was? How would she know when it was time to let him go out into the world and do whatever it was that God wanted him to do? How could she teach him to be a humble servant, even though he himself was God?

But no matter what she thought of the circumstance she faced, in the face of such questions and such dangers, Mary chose faith.

Responding to the words of Gabriel, Mary replied with the astonishing declaration: "Behold, I am the servant of the Lord; let it be to me according to your word" (Luke 1:38).

This remarkable response of trust in the goodness of God by a teenage girl is why this scenario is part of the Peter, Paul, and Mary principle.

THE TEMPLATE OF FAITH

Let's examine the events again against this principle of faith.

A. As we observed in the case of Peter and Paul, with Mary **it was God who sovereignly initiated the communication.** Almighty God dispatched the great archangel Gabriel to deliver the first news of the birth of the Messiah. Once again, because God is love, he communicates—and in this message, God was transmitting the ultimate gift of love, a Savior who would redeem mankind, destroy the works of the devil, and return the universe to complete perfection.

B. And just as with Peter and Paul, **Mary was frightened. We can imagine she questioned whether this was really a messenger from God.**

C. But like the other scenarios, here we see God's messenger putting the maiden at ease. **"Do not be afraid, Mary**, for you have found favor with God." Remember, peace is a key God has given to help us determine if a message is of God, of our own flesh, or of the devil.

D. **Mary wonders if this was, in fact, a messenger from God.** This could have been a deception sent from Satan. It could have been a hallucination brought on by an unexpected illness. But we see by Mary's response that she was confident this was truly God's will for her life.

E. The angel makes God's plan clear to Mary, **calling her to a higher level in life.**

F. Once she knows it is the will of God, **she now must decide** how she will respond. Faith wells up in Mary's heart and she decides to respond positively to God's plan for her life.

G. Now we come to the critical point where the leap is made from the spiritual into the natural. **Mary puts her belief into action by speaking** with her mouth this utterance of faith, "Let it be to me according to your word."

H. With this declaration the angel departs from her. We don't know when the Holy Spirit came to her, but when he overshadowed Mary as the angel foretold, the Peter, Paul, and Mary principle had its completion as **the Word of God was mixed with faith and corresponding action. Grace came on the scene and the miracle of the virgin conception occurred.**

THE MOTHER OF JOHN THE BAPTIST

We know Mary soon became pregnant because the Bible tells us she arose and went into the hill country with haste, to a city of Judah—likely to escape the sneers and derision by those in her village. When she arrived, Mary entered the house of Zacharias and greeted her relative Elizabeth, who was also pregnant, just as Gabriel had told her. When Mary greeted Elizabeth, the baby within the elderly lady leapt in her womb. At that moment, Elizabeth is filled with the Holy Spirit, and declares in a loud voice: "Blessed are you among women, and blessed is the fruit of your womb!" (Luke 1:42)

It needs to be noted here the Bible doesn't say Elizabeth had any foreknowledge of Mary's surprise pregnancy. The greeting is, in actuality, a prophetic utterance, and Mary most likely received it as a comforting reassurance this circumstance was of God.

> "And why is this granted to me that the mother of my Lord should come to me?" Elizabeth continued. "For behold, when the sound of your greeting came to my ears, the baby in my womb leaped for joy." (verses 43–44)

At this point we are given an important key to the Peter, Paul, and Mary principle. Elizabeth concluded her remarks by declaring, "And blessed is she who believed that there would be a fulfillment of what was spoken to her from the Lord" (v. 45).

Elizabeth was proclaiming an important truth. As the writer of Hebrew declares, "Now **faith** is the **assurance** of things **hoped for**, the **conviction** of things **not seen**" (Heb. 11:1 italics and emphasis added). As Jesus told his disciples, faith can move mountains. As we have already stated, faith is a vital element of our Christian walk.

You see, God is not impressed by religious platitudes that feign humility. Jesus made that clear in his dealings with the scribes and Pharisees. Those who know their God, they are the ones who will be strong, and they will do great exploits (Dan. 11:32). God wants bold and courageous followers who will dare to believe that the promises of God are yes, and then we add the amen of faith (2 Cor. 1:20).

ZECHARIAH AND A SECOND CHANCE

Elizabeth's household was facing its own test of faith. She and her husband Zechariah, who was a priest, were not able to conceive a child—a circumstance of shame in ancient Israel. Both were advanced in years, and they had long given up hope of ever having a child. Not long before Mary's visit, it had been Zechariah's honor and privilege to burn incense before the Lord in the temple. When the hour of service arrived, a multitude of people were gathered in the temple in prayer.

As Zechariah stood before the altar of the Lord, suddenly Gabriel, the same angel who spoke to Mary, appeared before him in the temple. Like Peter, Paul, and Mary, Zechariah was filled with fear, and he began to tremble. But the angel said to him, "Don't be afraid, Zechariah! God has heard your prayer. Your wife, Elizabeth, will give you a son, and you are to name him John. You will have great joy and gladness, and many will rejoice at his birth" (Luke 1:13–14 NLT).

Zechariah must have been dumbfounded by this message from heaven, but what Gabriel said next surely caused even greater bewilderment.

> For he will be great in the eyes of the Lord. He must never touch wine or other alcoholic drinks. He will be filled with the Holy Spirit, even before his birth. And he will turn many Israelites to the Lord their God. He will be a man with the spirit and power of Elijah. He will prepare the people for the coming of the Lord. (Luke 1:15–17 NLT)

The elderly priest was reeling from the message the angel brought to him. The words were wondrous. The promise seemed almost too good to be true. It was beyond belief. And that was precisely what Zechariah thought. Before he could stop himself, he blurted out the words, "How can this be? For I am an old man, and my wife is well advanced in years."

Though he was a priest in Israel, and he had stood in the very presence of God—and despite the fact this message was delivered by the most powerful of angels, in the very temple of God, Zechariah could not see past what he considered to be the practical limitations.

He just couldn't believe it.

The angel wasted no time in rebuking him for his lack of faith. "I am Gabriel!" he thundered. "I stand in the very presence of God. It was he who sent me to bring you this good news! But now, since you didn't believe what I said, you will be silent and unable to speak until the child is born. For my words will certainly be fulfilled at the proper time" (Luke 1:19-20 NLT).

So, when Zechariah emerged from the temple to the eagerly awaiting crowd, he was unable to speak—and they could tell he had seen a vision. As soon as his days of service at the temple were complete, the mute priest returned home.

It's interesting to observe the contrast between Zechariah's unbelieving reaction to the utterance of Gabriel, and Mary's response of faith. Zechariah was priest in the Abijah division, having served in the temple for years. He was well-versed in the Torah and in the religious traditions of the Jews. He was a man who commanded respect, as can be seen by the way the multitude waited with eager anticipation when he took so long to fulfill his duties at the altar of incense. The crowd was amazed at Zechariah's appearance, and they yearned to hear him tell what he had seen. He was an important man, with an important job, in the most important place for Jews on the face of this earth.

In contrast, Mary was a young woman from a tiny village in a scorned region of Israel called Nazareth of Galilee. She was untrained in the deeper truths of the Torah—that education was reserved for the young men. She lived in a time when women were regarded as second-hand citizens. Overall, women were expected to be the servants of men—to meet their needs, bear their children, take care of the mundane domestic duties, and stay out of the way.

But when the angel of the Lord appeared on the scene, it was the simple handmaiden of the Lord who responded in faith, and it was the educated religious leader who doubted. As a result of his unbelief, Zechariah received Gabriel's stinging rebuke, and the penalty of speechlessness. Mary, on the other hand, received God's blessing, and the praise of her cousin Elizabeth.

Wouldn't you like to receive the same commendation from the Lord? It's not always easy to believe God. One of my favorite Christian musicians, Steve Taylor, wrote a poignant song that highlighted the challenge of walking in faith, titled, "Harder to Believe Than Not To." Sometimes it seems God allows the circumstances of life to mount up on all sides of us just so in our helplessness, we will turn to him for salvation. The key to that intervention, though, is to keep our eyes on Jesus and his promises, and not on the wind and the waves of the adverse circumstances.

Remember, God is sovereign. He truly is in control of all the things that occur in our lives. He is well able to deliver us from any difficulty we face. There are two promises that should give us great comfort and expectation in this life. One is the declaration Gabriel made to Mary when referring to Elizabeth's miraculous pregnancy; "For nothing will be impossible with God." (Luke 1:37)

The other promise is taken from the words of Jesus in Mark 9:23, and while it may be hard for some to comprehend, it is equally true, "Anything is possible if a person believes" (Mark 9:23 NLT). We will discuss the tension between these truths further in the next chapter. But these Scriptures are central to our examination of Mary and Zechariah. Mary simply believed God could do what he said he was going to do—and God did it!

Mary remained with Elizabeth and Zechariah for three months, more than likely helping with the household duties so her elderly cousin could rest and allow the baby to fully develop in her womb. There is no doubt she heard the story of Zechariah's encounter with Gabriel in the temple. The priest may have scribbled the story onto a tablet, and Elizabeth relayed it to her teen-aged cousin. I suspect Mary shared her own angelic and miraculous encounter with Elizabeth and Zechariah, which may have been shocking to the priest. But after hearing Elizabeth's confession of how the baby in her womb was filled with the Holy Spirit, and leapt within her at Mary's greeting, Zechariah's heart may have been softened.

We don't know when his doubt turned to faith, but the Bible tells us not long after Mary returned to Nazareth, Elizabeth gave birth to a boy. When her neighbors and friends heard how the Lord had shown great mercy, they rejoiced with her, just as the angel had said. On the eighth day, according to the Jewish law, they came to the synagogue to circumcise the child. Now the town leaders assumed after these many years of bareness, the elderly couple would surely name the child Zechariah after his father. But Elizabeth was firm in her declaration of the child's name—he would be named John, just as the angel had said.

The leaders of the synagogue were shocked at her bold statement. They may have thought she was forgetting her place with such a reply. "There is no one among your relatives who is called by that name." Brushing her aside, they approached Zechariah. "What would you have him called," they asked, no doubt assuming he would agree with them. Zechariah asked them to give him a writing tablet. Slowly, methodically, he scribbled the words, "His name is John," just as the angel had said. (Luke 1:59–63 NLT)

Immediately his mouth was opened, and his tongue loosed, and he spoke, praising God. Then fear came on all who dwelled around them; and all these things spread throughout the hill country of Judea. Everyone who heard of it wondered, and asked, "What kind of child will this be?" The Bible tells us the hand of the Lord was with Zechariah and Elizabeth's little boy John from that day forward—just as the angel had said.

This little boy would grow to become the man we know as John the Baptist—the final Old Testament prophet who declared the coming of the Messiah, his cousin, Jesus Christ.

I share the rest of the story with you because it's important to recognize even great and respected religious leaders like Zechariah sometimes fail in employing the Peter, Paul, and Mary principle in their own lives. And yet, as we see in this story, our loving heavenly Father is the God of second chances. His mercies are new every morning.

Zechariah failed initially in his encounter with God, but he was given a chance for redemption. The second time around he got it right. God gave a second chance for a faithful response from Zechariah, and he will give us a second chance as well.

Mary, Joseph, and a Response of Faith

After Mary left Zechariah and Elizabeth she returned to Nazareth where she had to confront another crisis of faith. At some point Joseph, her betrothed, was informed of the pregnancy. The Bible tells us he planned to break off the betrothal. But Joseph was a merciful man, and so he planned to divorce Mary quietly so she would not be stoned to death (Matthew 1:19). Though he may have been angry, embarrassed, and confused at the announcement of her pregnancy, he was not going to seek vengeance—that was in the hands of the Lord.

But God had another plan. One night, Joseph fell asleep as he wrestled with his decision concerning his betrothal. As he slept, an angel of the Lord appeared to him in a dream, bringing words of comfort. "Joseph, son of David," the angel said, "do not be afraid to take Mary as your wife. For the child within her was conceived by the Holy Spirit" (Matthew 1:20 NLT). The angel gave the same information to Joseph that he had given to Mary. "And she will have a son, and you are to name him Jesus, for he will save his people from their sins" (Matthew 1:21 NLT).

Like Mary, Joseph chose faith. Matthew tells us Joseph, being aroused from sleep, did as the angel of the Lord commanded him, and took to himself his wife. Can you imagine what kind of wedding that must have been? Perhaps Zechariah, Elizabeth, and baby John traveled to Nazareth for the ceremony? One must wonder what kinds of speeches were made by the father of the bride or by the leader of the synagogue.

One of my favorite lines in the excellent Christmas movie, *The Nativity Story*, is uttered by Joseph as they travel to Bethlehem for the census. "I wonder if I will be able to teach him anything at all?"

Can you imagine being the parents of the Son of God?

Within a short period of time, Joseph and Mary arrived in Bethlehem to be registered in the census. And there, in a cave that doubled as a stable for the innkeeper's animals, the Messiah, the Promised One of the Father, the Creator of the Universe, and the Savior of all mankind was born; a baby destined to sit on the throne of his father, David; and a King whose reign would have no end—just as the angel had said.

—CHAPTER FIVE—
FAITH IN THE LIFE OF JESUS

The teaching and techniques of Rabbi Jesus of Nazareth were like nothing ever seen before. He is a truly unique figure in human history. But we can't stop there because he is also the Son of God. There is a common misunderstanding about how Jesus operated while living on planet earth. It's important to understand in addition to being the Son of God, Jesus was also the Son of Man—fully God and fully human at the same time. While he didn't lose his divine nature when he was born in Bethlehem, he did temporarily relinquish his glory and power.

There are quaint stories of Jesus performing miracles as a child, but these are not found in Scripture. It's significant to note that Scripture does not report Jesus doing any miracles until he was water baptized at the age of thirty after the Holy Spirit came upon him. It was the Holy Spirit that gave him the power to perform the miracles. There are two vital things we need to learn from this truth. First, the power of God flows through the Holy Spirit. While fully God, Jesus had "emptied himself" of his divine power and glory during his earthly ministry, according to Philippians 2:7. "although He existed in the form of God, did not regard equality with God a thing to be grasped, but emptied

Himself, taking the form of a bond-servant, and being made in the likeness of men." (Philippians 2:6-7, NASB).

Theologian, Dr. J. Rodman Williams writes of Philippians 2:7: "What exactly did He empty Himself of? Paul's words in Philippians 2:7 are to be understood as Christ's surrender of His glory and riches in the taking on the form of a servant or slave. The self-emptying was a profound expression of the love and compassion that is the central reality of God's nature." The full glory of God during Jesus earthly ministry was only shown to the three apostles on the mount of transfiguration (Matthew 17). The rest of the time he walked the earth without that glory and only performed miracles after his baptism when the Holy Spirit had come upon him.[1]

Dr. Daniel Gilbert of Regent University Divinity School observes, "Jesus did not lay down His divinity, He took up humanity."[2]

We see Jesus' baptism in Luke chapter 3, then Luke emphasized the point in chapter 4, verse 1: "And Jesus, **full of the Holy Spirit**, returned from the Jordan and was led by the Spirit in the wilderness... (Luke 4:1 ESV, emphasis added). After overcoming the temptation of the devil in the wilderness Luke describes Jesus's first recorded public sermon. Once again, Luke emphasized that "Jesus returned **in the power of the Spirit**." (Luke 4:14 ESV, emphasis added). Entering his hometown of Nazareth, Jesus is invited to read from the Torah. Luke records the significant words spoken by Christ as he embarked on his earthly ministry.

"He unrolled the scroll and found the place where it was written, 'The Spirit is upon me, because he has anointed me to proclaim good news to the poor. He sent me to proclaim liberty to the captives and recovering of sight to the blind, to set at liberty those who are oppressed, to proclaim the year of the Lord's favor.'" (Luke 4:17-19 ESV)

While Jesus was fully God, he was also fully human. In his earthly ministry, he had to be empowered by the Holy Spirit before he could do any miracles. In the same way, we must be filled with the Holy Spirit to experience the power of God in our lives.

Second, Jesus had to have faith in the goodness and promises of the Father to walk in miracles. So too, we must have faith to receive from God for ourselves and for others. Our goal in this life is to strive to become more and more like Jesus. So, if faith was at the center of his life, then we should seek for it to be at the center of ours. The apostle Paul makes this clear when he writes:

> For God knew his people in advance, and he chose them to **become like his Son**, so that his Son would be the firstborn among many brothers and sisters. (Romans 8:29 NLT, italics and emphasis added)

And also:

> This will continue until we all come to such unity in our faith and knowledge of God's Son that we will be mature in the Lord, **measuring up to the full and complete standard of Christ**. (Ephesians 4:13 NLT, italics and emphasis added)

The apostle John confirmed what Paul taught when he wrote this remarkable statement:

> So we will not be afraid on the day of judgment, but we can face him with confidence because **we live like Jesus here in this world**. (1 John 4:17 NLT, italics and emphasis added)

JESUS RESPONDS TO FAITH—OR A LACK OF IT

As I explained in the first chapter, the gospel writers make it clear Jesus responded to faith. He marveled both at the faith of the Roman centurion (Matt. 8:5–13) and at the lack of faith of those from his hometown who saw him only as Joe and Mary's boy (Mark 6:1-6).

In his teaching and in his example, Jesus made it abundantly clear faith is the currency of heaven. Throughout the gospels, he is either praising people for their faith (the key to receiving from God) or admonishing them for their lack of faith.

It's important to understand the motive behind Jesus's responses. He was not angry at his disciples when they lacked faith. Instead, like a father who is helping a child to learn a vital skill for living—like riding a bike, driving a car, or doing a budget—Jesus is trying to help them see the vital importance of faith in our interaction with heaven.

Again and again, he repeats the lesson:

> If God cares so wonderfully for flowers that are here today and thrown in the fire tomorrow, he will certainly care for you? **Why do you have so little faith!** (Matthew 6:30 NLT, italics and emphasis added)

> And he said to him, "Rise and go your way; **your faith has made you well.**" (Luke 17:19, italics and emphasis added)

> And he said to them, "Why are you afraid, O **you of little faith**?" Then he rose and rebuked the winds and the sea, and there was a great calm. (Matthew 8:26, italics and emphasis added)

> And they brought to Him a paralyzed man lying on a stretcher. And **seeing their faith**, Jesus said to the man who was paralyzed, "Take courage, son; your sins are forgiven." (Matthew 9:2 NASB, italics and emphasis added)

> And Jesus said to him, "Regain your sight; **your faith has made you well.**" (Luke 18:42 NASB, italics and emphasis added)

If you believe the Bible is the revealed will of God, there is no escaping it—faith is the currency of heaven. We receive everything from God by faith.

In Mark 11:22, Jesus emphatically declared to his disciples, "Have faith in God." Then he went on to describe the kind of faith he was talking about. "Truly, I say to you, whoever says to this mountain, 'Be taken up and thrown into the sea,' and does not doubt in his heart, but believes that what he says will come to pass, It will be done for him. Therefore I tell you, whatever you ask in pray, **believe that you have received it.** and it will be yours" (Mark 11:23-24).

This is a remarkable statement from Jesus—it almost seems like Jesus was speaking in total hyperbole. But when we understand the fullness of the Peter, Paul, and Mary principle and how biblical faith truly operates, we comprehend what Jesus is saying. We will discuss this further in the next chapter.

Faith Working in the Ministry of Jesus

The gospel writers share other remarkable encounters with Jesus where people had conditions that were impossible to remedy at that time in history, and yet these people were healed. In each case, Jesus made it clear they were healed due to their faith. First, let's read about the woman who was healed of uncontrollable bleeding.

> A great crowd followed him and thronged about him. And there was a woman who had had a discharge of blood for twelve years, and who had suffered much under many physicians, and had spent all that she had, and was no better but rather grew worse. She had heard the reports about Jesus and came up behind him in the crowd and touched his garment. For she said, "If I touch even his garments, I will be made well."
>
> And immediately the flow of blood dried up, and she felt in her body that she was healed of her disease. And

> Jesus, perceiving in himself that power had gone out from him, immediately turned about in the crowd and said, "Who touched my garments?" And his disciples said to him, "You see the crowd pressing around you, and yet you say, 'Who touched me?'" And he looked around to see who had done it.
>
> But the woman, knowing what had happened to her, came in fear and trembling and fell down before him and told him the whole truth. And he said to her, "Daughter, **your faith has made you well**; go in peace, and be healed of your disease." (Mark 5:24–34, italics and emphasis added)

Another powerful example is when Jesus heals ten lepers—but only one comes back to thank him.

> As he entered a village, he was met by ten lepers, who stood at a distance and lifted up their voices, saying, "Jesus, Master, have mercy on us." When he saw them, he said to them, "Go and show yourselves to the priests." And as they went, they were cleansed.
>
> Then one of them, when he saw that he was healed, turned back, praising God with a loud voice; and he fell on his face at Jesus' feet, giving him thanks. Now he was a Samaritan. Then Jesus answered, "Were not ten cleansed? Where are the nine? Was no one found to return and give praise to God except this foreigner?" And he said to him, "Rise and go your way; **your faith has made you well**." (Luke 17:12–19, italics and emphasis added)

Jesus could not have been clearer in his response to these hurting people. He said plainly, "Your faith has made you well." What is the thread that runs through the Peter, Paul, and Mary principle? Believing God and his Word.

GROWING IN FAITH

The disciples could see walking in faith was the key to both power and provision from God—and they knew they were lacking in their faith. One day the apostles said to the Lord, The apostles said to the Lord, "Show us how to increase our faith" (Luke 17:5 NLT). Jesus's response startled them. "The Lord answered, 'If you had faith even as small as a mustard seed, you could say to this mulberry tree, 'May you be uprooted and be planted in the sea,' and it would obey you!'" (Luke 17:6 NLT).

Jesus wanted his followers then and now to know it doesn't take the faith of a mature pastor, evangelist, or missionary to receive from God. Even faith the size of a mustard seed—one of the smallest seeds in the world—is effective to move those things that seem like mountains in your life.

You might say, "I don't know if I even have mustard seed-sized faith." If you care whether you have enough faith, then *you do have enough faith*! The apostle Paul declared this of every believer:

> God has allotted to each ***a measure of faith***. (Romans 12:3 NASB, italics and emphasis added)

God gives to each of us our first seedlings of faith. Faith enough for us to receive the greatest miracle we could ever know—our salvation through Jesus. If we can receive that, we can receive anything God intends for us to have in this life. Then as we walk in relationship with God, and as we read his Word, our faith begins to grow. Paul explains:

> Faith comes from hearing, and hearing through the word of Christ. (Romans 10:17)

As we study and meditate on the Bible, the Holy Spirit gives us understanding and revelation to know him better. As we spend time in prayer, worship, and fellowship with other believers we grow stronger and stronger in our faith. By walking in these Christian disciplines, we are planting those mustard seeds and watering them. Over time they grow into a mustard plant and then into a mustard tree of faith!

FAITH IN OUR LIVES

The truth is that we often take natural faith for granted. Most people don't have a second thought that a high-rise building will continue to stand, that an airplane will take off and land safely, that bridges will carry our cars from one side to another, and that tunnels will not collapse. In many ways, it takes tremendous faith to drive a car on a busy highway, or even cross the street in front of your house.

Yet when it comes to receiving the promises of God, many people are at a loss. Like earthly confidence, biblical faith is about believing, and then acting on that belief. It is being assured the promises God gave in the Bible are true. It is also being confident the promises God makes directly to us are also true, and he is faithful to see them fulfilled in our lives.

Understanding the Peter, Paul, and Mary principle helps us as we grow in our relationship with the Lord as we remember:

- God initiates the growth of your faith. The fact you're reading this book is confirmation he is working to bring you what you need to grow in your relationship with him.
- As he reveals new aspects of his Word, you may feel stretched or even anxious as you learn to walk in faith in that area.
- As he gently leads you onward by his Holy Spirit, you will come to a place of sensing his peace.
- In this process you may question whether this part of Scripture is for today, or maybe even if this part of the Bible is truly from God.

- God will bring confirmation through various means to confirm his Word is true and to call you to a higher place in him.
- You will have to decide to trust his promises and precepts to grow or to stay where you are.
- Once you've decided, you will need to act in faith—pulling that thing from the spirit/soul realm into the natural realm.
- When you act in faith on the revelation of God's Word, grace comes on the scene and God moves mightily in your life. When you experience this process and see God's mighty power in your life, your faith grows—and so does your love for your heavenly Father.

Now let's see how the Peter, Paul, and Mary principle unfolds in practical ways in our everyday lives.

—CHAPTER SIX—
FAITH IN ACTION

A common expression relates directly to the Peter, Paul, and Mary principle: "You can become so heavenly minded, you are no earthly good." Some Christians become so spiritually-minded while reading their Bible, praying, or spending time in worship—all excellent spiritual disciplines, mind you—they forget we are also called to reach out in love to other people in the name of Jesus. While prayer, worship, and scriptural meditation is part of the Christian life, it is not the whole of it. As we already quoted from James, "faith without works is dead."

The Bible tells us that we are created for the purpose of doing good works:

> For we are His workmanship, created in Christ Jesus for good works, which God prepared beforehand, that we should walk in them. (Ephesians 2:10 NASB)

God has designed us with certain talents and abilities that will allow us to fulfill this purpose. He has a blueprint for our lives that is part of his greater plan of revealing his love to this fallen world.

To ensure we are not confused, by the leading of the Holy Spirit, Paul places this passage directly after the verse that makes clear *our salvation is not gained by works, but by grace through faith.*

> For by grace you have been saved through faith; and this is not of yourselves, it is the gift of God; not a result of works, so that no one should boast. (Ephesians 2:8–9 NASB)

This is what sets Christianity apart from every other religion in the world. As disciples of Jesus, we know we can never be good enough or do enough good works to earn salvation. Our redemption comes only through faith in the sacrifice of Jesus on the cross.

Instead, the Bible makes clear our good works are a byproduct of our salvation—they flow from a heart of love and thanksgiving. We love others because God first loved us.

Returning to the passage in James, we see the works spoken of here are not to secure salvation (spirit/soul realm), but to demonstrate our love for God outwardly (natural realm) for what God has done for us.

Again, it's helpful to remember Jesus was a Jewish rabbi. He taught the abstract concepts to his disciples, but then he sent them out to put them into practice with these instructions:

> Go and announce to them that the Kingdom of Heaven is near. ... Give as freely as you have received! (Matthew 10:7–8 NLT)

In sending out his disciples, Jesus was demonstrating to all believers for all time that our assignment is to go and to do. Paul makes this clear when he declares: "For we are God's fellow workers" (1 Corinthians 3:9 NASB).

In another passage, Jesus gives us this remarkable statement:

> Truly, truly, I say to you, he who believes in me will also do the works that I do; and greater works than these he will do, because I am going to the Father. (John 14:12)

His final instructions to his disciples—and to all believers—before ascending into heaven is known as the Great Commission.

> Go therefore and make disciples of all nations, baptizing them in the name of the Father and of the Son and of the Holy Spirit, teaching them to observe all I have commanded you. And behold, I am with you always, to the end of the age. (Matthew 28:19-20)

I had the privilege of ministering with Gordon Robertson of *The 700 Club* in various settings for several years. I often heard him say of the Great Commission: "What part of 'go ye' don't you understand. 'Go' means move out from where you are, and 'ye' means you!"

Someone has said that to fulfill God's plan for our lives, we must consider the "Three Ds"—discover, develop, and deploy:

- Discover God's will and how to operate in his ways,
- Develop the talents and spiritual gifts God has given to us,
- Deploy—or go out and do that which God has created you for in your lifetime.

FROM HEAVEN TO EARTH

The writer of Hebrews gives us an important definition of biblical faith and an explanation of how it operates between heaven and earth.

> Now faith is the **substance** of things **hoped** for, the **evidence** of things **not seen**. (Hebrews 11:1 NKJV, italics and emphasis added)

Earlier, we explained the important concept that by operating in the Peter, Paul, and Mary principle, the believer reaches into the spirit realm and receives the promises of Scripture by faith. There is always a spiritual beginning and a natural ending in the PP&M process. Let's examine this passage to gain further understanding.

The first key word, *faith* is *pistis* in Greek. According to *Strong's Concordance*, pistis means, "conviction of the truth of anything, or belief; in the New Testament of a conviction or belief respecting man's relationship to God and divine things." The Geneva Bible notes give further insight into this verse: "An excellent description of faith by the effects, because it represents things which are but yet in hope and sets as it were before our eyes things that are invisible."

The next key word is *substance*, which is part of the natural world. The Greek word is *hupostasis*, which means "that which has foundation, is firm, or that which has actual existence." The writer is saying that 'faith' (which is from the spirit/soul realm) is the 'substance' (from the natural realm) of things 'hoped for' (once again, from the spirit/soul realm).

Like all good Hebrew teachers, the writer repeats the concept in different terms: it is the *evidence*, which in Greek is *elegchos*, meaning "that by which a thing is proved or tested" (the natural realm) of things not seen (spirit/soul realm).

Let's see how the meeting of the spirit/soul realm and the natural realm fits into the Peter, Paul, and Mary principle:

A. God initiates the communication (spirit/soul realm).
B. The believer hears the voice of God and is filled with fear, confusion, or anxiety (spirit/soul).
C. God brings his peace (spirit/soul).
D. The believer wonders if it really is God communicating or if it is just his or her own mind (spirit/soul).

E. God always calls the believer to a higher level (spirit/soul).

F. The believer recognizes the communication is from God and must decide (spirit/soul).

G. Once a decision is made there must be corresponding action, ***taking the experience from the spiritual into the natural realm.***

H. In faith (spirit/soul), action is taken (natural realm). At that moment, the grace of God comes on the scene, mixing with the Word of God and the faith of the disciple (spirit/soul realm). Then in God's time and in his way, he answers the prayer, and that thing is received by the believing person (concluding in the natural realm).

God Rules!

In all of this we must remember God is in control. He is the Creator and Sustainer of all things. The Bible declares:

> He existed before anything else, and he holds all creation together. (Colossians 1:17 NLT)

In humility, we must acknowledge God is not a vending machine. Instead, he is a loving heavenly Father who wants to bring blessing to us and our families—and through us to the people of the world. We may ask for something in prayer he does not desire for us to have. When that is the case, we can gratefully thank God for his wisdom. Most of us have experienced times when we didn't receive our desired answer in prayer, and later, we realized God was protecting us from something we were unaware of.

Just like a natural parent, God wants to bless us with good things—but not all we ask for in prayer is for our ultimate good.

He has revealed the elements of the Peter, Paul, and Mary principle to show his love, to both encourage and equip disciples, and also to lead the lost to salvation. You and I are his hands, feet, and voice in the earth—a conduit of his love and mercy to hurting people everywhere.

Through his interactions with Peter, Paul, and Mary, we can see how the Lord intervened in the affairs of humans to forward his purposes in the earth. God's ultimate purpose is to reveal himself to all people to redeem them through his Son. He can fulfill his purpose any way he desires. He is God. This is his creation, whether we acknowledge his ownership or not.

> The earth is the LORD's, and everything in it. The world and all its people belong to him. (Psalm 24:1 NLT)

God set creation in motion—and the subsequent epochs of man's existence. It is "his-story." In other words, God is sovereign. Or as I used to say when I traveled with a Christian rock band, "God rules!" Ultimately, his plans will be fulfilled in the earth.

"So why do I have to concern myself with faith?" you may wonder. "If God's plan is going to come to pass anyway, why do I need to be worried about how I respond to his guidance in my life?"

As we saw in the case of Zechariah, if we don't respond in faith to God's directives, there can be negative consequences for us and our families. There could possibly be negative consequences for our communities or beyond, depending on our influence. One of the negative consequences is God's blessing is not released to us, our families, or our communities.

So, what happens if we don't respond in faith? God looks for another person through whom he can release his blessing. An instructive example of this is the father of Abram (Abraham), a man named Terah. The writer of Genesis tells the story:

> Now Terah took Abram his son, and Lot the son of Haran, his grandson, and Sarai his daughter-in-law, his son Abram's wife; and they departed together from Ur of the Chaldeans to go the land of Canaan; and they went as far as Haran and settled there. And the days of Terah were two hundred and five years; and Terah died in Haran. Genesis 11:31–32 NASB)

One of the things I've learned about screenwriting is in a good movie every scene has a purpose in the end. It's the same with Bible study. Everything we read in the Bible is there for a reason. For some reason, the Holy Spirit revealed through these passages that Terah's plan was to leave Ur of the Chaldeans and to enter the land of Canaan. However, he traveled as far as a place called Haran and stopped. We don't know why he did not proceed to Canaan, but we do know Terah settled and eventually died in Haran.

Why is this significant? In the very next verse, we are given a glimpse into God's plan:

> Now the Lord said to Abram, "Go forth from your country, and from your relatives and from your father's house, to the land which I will show you. (Genesis 12:1 NASB)

Verse 5 tells us Abram packed everything and moved to Canaan—the place his father had originally chosen as a destination. After arriving in Canaan, God appeared to Abram and said, "'To your descendants I will give this land'" (Genesis 12:7 NASB).

Though it is not explicitly stated, these passages imply God intended to give this promise to Terah. In the previous chapter we see Terah's son, Haran, had died suddenly (Genesis 11). Terah stopped his forward motion and settled in a place of the same name, Haran, where he eventually died. Perhaps Terah was so overcome by grief he gave up on God's plan, settled someplace and named it after his dead son. Instead of burying his dead son and moving on in obedience to God's call, Terah likely remained in sorrow and never saw the fulfilment of God's plan for him and his entire family.

What did God do in response to Terah's lack of faith and corresponding action? He searched for another who would respond in faith. He found that person in Terah's son, Abram—who, because of his faith and action, would become Abraham, the father of faith.

By acting in faith, like Abram, we open the door to God's blessing in our lives. By neglecting to act on the call of God for our lives, we can find ourselves mourning in the desert and never walking in the abundant life God intends for us.

It's like God has packed his celestial minivan full of presents (use your imagination on this one), and he has delivered them to our front door. He has announced his intention to give the gifts to you and is ringing the doorbell. But unless we open the door through faith and corresponding action, those gifts will remain unwrapped on our doorstep—even though it's God's intention we bring them into our home, unwrap them, and put them to use.

Faith in Everyday Life

As you can see, walking in faith is not merely a spiritual practice, but a practical and normal part of life for the New Testament disciple. Faith leads to a victorious Christian life. Many Christians read the words of Jesus from John 10:10, "I came so that they would have life, and have it abundantly," and wonder what abundant life looks like. They wonder why they don't seem to be living in this abundance.

My first response is we need to be careful in defining the word "abundance". Some have associated "abundance" with material wealth and possessions. I'm not convinced Jesus was referring to material wealth when he spoke of living abundantly. The Bible speaks of many godly people who were wealthy—including the father of faith, Abraham. The Scripture also tells of many who did not have financial wealth. There is no Scripture that explicitly connects abundance with money or material possessions. Conversely, there are several passages that warn against "the love of money", which the apostle Paul defines as "the root of all evil." He goes on to warn "It is through this craving that some have wandered away from the faith and pierced themselves through with many pangs" (1 Timothy 6:10).

When considering the definition of abundant life, I believe there are three basic classifications of people; Pay-ers, Pray-ers, and Play-ers.

The Pay-ers: Some people are gifted by God with the ability to make money. I believe these people have a responsibility to do good with their wealth by building businesses and organizations to employ people, funding local churches and ministries, supporting world missions, giving to important charitable endeavors, and investing in research and development to improve the lives of others and help to solve pressing problems faced by humanity.

The Pray-ers: These are intercessors and worker bees. These folks are often in the background, quietly lifting up prayers and petitions to God and giving unseen service to support the ministry or outreach. Because the Bible tells us to pray privately, they don't often shine as "leaders" in a church or ministry—but they shine like stars in the eyes of God.

Prayer is the foundation upon which any ministry thrives. The pray-ers are the most overlooked and undervalued part of most ministries—and perhaps the most essential.

The Play-ers: The final group is the play-ers—these are the vocational ministers who give their lives in service to the Lord. These are the Billy Grahams and the Mother Teresas of this world. But they are also the unknown and unnamed missionaries, Christian school teachers, homeschool parents, pastors, elders, apostles, Bible college professors and administrators, evangelists, prophets, para-church ministers, television evangelists, internet evangelists, and more.

They are people who have counted the cost, picked up their cross, laid down their lives, and followed Christ no matter what is required of them.

If it is only the play-ers doing the work of the ministry—as it is in some churches and organizations—then multitudes of people will never have the opportunity to hear the gospel message. Why? Because it is a mathematical impossibility. There are not enough people in full-time ministry to reach the billions of lost people in the world—even with the advent of modern modes of communication like television, radio, and the internet. It will take the entire body of Christ, working in unity and following the direction of Jesus to see the Great Commission accomplished.

The play-ers need the support of the pay-ers and the pray-ers for their ministry to be effective. In fact, without the pay-ers and the pray-ers, the play-ers would be severely limited, if not completely constricted, from doing what God has called them to do.

To a certain degree, we are all three at various times in our lives. But each of us is called to excel as a pay-er, a pray-er, or a play-er. We can ask God to show us which one is our main calling. When he answers that question, follow that course with diligence, asking the Lord to lead you and to bless the work of your hands.

Seed Faith to Tree Faith

Now that you understand the necessity of faith for a victorious Christian life, it's important to know how faith grows. The apostle Paul declares, "Faith comes by hearing, and hearing by the Word of God" (Romans 10:17). In the parable of the sower, Jesus describes the Word of God as a seed that grows when sown in the good soil of a believer's heart. As that seed is watered and nurtured, it grows little by little.

Soon that mustard seed is a mustard tree of faith, bringing life to all around it. As we "hear" the Word of God and then act in faith on those scriptural promises, we see and experience God's faithfulness. This process gives us confidence to step out further and further in faith as it is needed in life. As we continue in this process of trial and error, exploring the things of God and getting to know his character and attributes, our faith continues to grow.

Faith is not only believing God *can*, it's knowing he *will*—if it be his will. Knowing God's Word leads to knowing his will—and then to doing his will.

In Jesus's teaching on the parable of the talents, he declared: "The one who is faithful in a very little is also faithful in much" (Luke 16:10). Faith in the little things leads to faith in the big things. The Bible says, "Don't despise the days of small beginnings" (Zechariah 4:10 NLT). Start where you are. Step out in faith, believing the promise of God concerning something you may need in your life. You will likely be amazed as you see God move to show his faithfulness to you in that area.

Take a moment right now to think about something you need. Find the promise of God concerning that thing in the Scripture. Now write down a declaration of faith about that thing on the lines on the next page and add the date.

_____

_____

_____

_____

Now, day by day, continue to thank God for answering your prayer and providing for your need in this area of your life. Faith is the key to being effective as a servant of God. It allows you to do more than you think you can do—to dream big for God, for his people, for the kingdom, and for the world. As Bible teacher Larry Tomczak often says, "Step out of your ability and step into God's ability." Faith helps us to step outside ourselves where our own selfish desires are no longer in control.

We don't need more of God; we have all of Christ we will ever require—what we need is less of ourselves.

DIVINE REJECTIONS

It's important to remember God will answer our prayers—and sometimes not answer our prayers—according to his will and plan for our lives. There will be times when we ask for something in prayer, standing in faith on the promises of God, and he will either say no to the request or answer the prayer in a way we are not expecting. This kind of response from heaven is often called a "divine rejection."

A divine rejection is like the fish that is somehow diverted from going after the worm with the hook in it. The fish may truly desire the worm but certainly does not desire the hook. There are things we earnestly desire, but only God knows if there is a hook hidden behind the object of our affection. We may mourn for a time that God didn't answer our prayer the way we wanted him to, but we may never know until we reach heaven how many times he saved us from the hidden hook.

BELIEVE AND RECEIVE

In the Gospel of Mark, Jesus makes a remarkable statement about faith:

> Therefore I tell you, whatever you ask in prayer, believe that you have received it, and it will be yours. (Mark 11:24)

At first glance this passage seems to be outside the realm of reality and simply a statement of hyperbole by Jesus to make a point. Some call this "name it and claim it" faith. We've made it clear God is not a slot machine, and prayer is not heavenly quarters. And yet this passage would almost lead us to believe we can have anything we ask for in prayer if we believe God will answer. So, what is Jesus saying here and how can we apply it to our lives?

You will recall our discussion about the positive response of Jesus to those exhibiting faith. He clearly said several times to those seeking healing, "Your faith has made you well." The writer of Hebrews brings some clarity by declaring, "Without faith it is impossible to please God" (Hebrews 11:6 NLT). God is pleased when we walk in faith because it opens the door for him to bless us—and through us to bless others. Our heavenly Father loves to lavish gifts on his children just as an earthly father does. So, when Jesus declares that "whatever you ask in prayer, believe that you have received it, and it will be yours," I believe he is encouraging his disciples—then and now—to ask big, to think big, to be audacious in their belief because that kind of faith would open the door for our heavenly Father to pour out his blessings to us and through us.

At the same time, this statement is tempered by Jesus's earthly life. In everything, Jesus is our example, so it's helpful to consider how he walked in faith during his time on the earth. In the most challenging moments of his life, as he struggled with the faith and obedience necessary for him to go to the cross, Jesus gives an amazing demonstration of faith. Like his mother, Mary, who questioned God's plan while still maintaining her faith, Jesus does the same in the Garden of Gethsemane. Facing not only torture and an excruciating death on the cross, but also separation from his Father for the first and only time in eternal history, Jesus prays an agonizing prayer of faith. "Father, if You are willing, remove this cup from Me; yet not My will, but Yours be done" (Luke 22:42 NASB).

This is true faith—to make a request from the desire of one's heart and yet to be willing to cooperate with God's ultimate will, even if it will require sacrifice, pain, or loss.

I will say here I don't believe in "name it and claim it" faith. What I do believe in is "hear it, name it, and claim it" faith.

So, what is the difference? In so called "name it and claim" theology, the person randomly "names" and "claims" something God might not intend for them to have. Instead of seeking God's plan, they simply extend faith for whatever they want. This is like the old story of the gunman who shoots a hole in the side of the barn and then paints a bullseye around the hole—it is meaningless. The true sharpshooter aims at a target and then shoots through the center of the bullseye.

This is what I believe Jesus is communicating in this verse from the Gospel of Mark. Through an ongoing relationship with God, we discern the leading of the Holy Spirit concerning a matter. True disciples of Jesus humble themselves, seeking God's will. They have not only received

Jesus as Savior, but also as Lord of their life. Like John the Baptist, they have determined that "He must increase, but I must decrease" (John 3:30). As a result of their relationship with God, they sense his direction as they pray. Their desire is for their heart to come into alignment with the heart of God. So, after having heard from God, they ask in faith, believing they will receive the thing God has already promised by the leading of the Holy Spirit.

They "hear it, name it, and claim it"—and when they receive the answer to their prayer their faith grows even more.

SHADRACH, MESCHACH AND ABEDNEGO FAITH

We see an important example of true biblical faith in the Hebrew exiles, Shadrach, Meschach, and Abednego, as they face the wrath of King Nebuchadnezzar for not bowing to his golden idol. Faced with death in the fiery furnace, these three men of faith made a bold proclamation before this earthly king.

> If it be so, our God whom we serve is able to deliver us from the furnace of blazing fire; and He will deliver us out of your hand, O king. **But even if He does not**, let it be known to you, O king, that we are not going to serve your gods or worship the golden statue that you have set up. (Daniel 3:17–18 NASB, italics and emphasis added)

Filled with rage at their disobedience to his decree, Nebuchadnezzar had the three men bound and thrown into the fire. Miraculously, the flames did not consume them. The king of Babylon was so amazed by this miracle he immediately declared:

> Blessed be the God of Shadrach, Meshach and Abednego, who has sent His angel and delivered His servants who put their trust in Him ... there is no other god who is able to save in this way. (Daniel 3:28–29 NASB)

True faith does not focus on self, but always glorifies God and seeks his plan and purpose above all. That is the faith of the Peter, Paul, and Mary principle.

Now that you understand how the principle works in the life of the believer, it is time to apply it in practical ways in your life. In part two, we will examine key biblical doctrines and apply the principle to see how you can receive these blessings in your life.

—CHAPTER SEVEN—
FAITH FOR SALVATION

When I first saw this principle of faith in the lives of Peter, Paul, and Mary, I thought it was an interesting spiritual discovery, but I wondered if it could be applied in modern life. As I prayed about this, I sensed the Holy Spirit leading me to apply the principle to our salvation experience. Let's take a look.

A. **God initiated the communication.**

As sons of Adam and daughters of Eve, each of us inherit the sin nature from birth. We are dead in our sins and captive to our carnal nature. We are merely looking to please ourselves and we are certainly not looking for God. But in his mercy, God reaches out to us through the gentle leading of the Holy Spirit. The apostle Paul writes of our condition when he observes:

> Oh, what a miserable person I am! Who will free me from this life that is dominated by sin and death? (Romans 7:24 NLT)

But then Paul also gives us this glimpse into the mercy of God for us in our fallen condition.

> But God showed his great love for us by sending Christ to die for us while we were still sinners. (Romans 5:8 NLT)

B. **Man hears the voice and is filled with fear, confusion, and anxiety.**

In our fallen state, we are separated from God. We don't know him. We don't understand his ways. Some think if he exists, he is a moral monster for allowing the suffering in this world to take place. Others don't think he exists, and so, they ignore him and go about their lives as if they are a god unto themselves. The world exists for them and their pleasure.

But when our loving heavenly Father begins to invade our lives and make his presence known, our world is turned upside down. For those who believe in a higher power, they grapple with who this deity could be. In confusion and anxiety, they search for answers.

It's even worse for the atheist who suddenly understands there is a spiritual universe with a powerful God. The famous writer and theologian C. S. Lewis had been an atheist, but the Holy Spirit began to reveal the reality of God and the spirit world to him little by little. Lewis later confessed when he started to realize there really is a God, it was like the mouse who realizes there really is a cat.

C. **God brings his peace.**

You may remember the moment in your salvation experience where the peace of God flooded your soul. It may have been just an overall sense of well-being. Peace is a key indicator that God is in the situation. Peace is one of the fruits of the Spirit (Galatians 5:22–23).

Peace is also one of the keys to God's guidance in our lives. The prophet Isaiah declares:

> For you will go out with joy, And be led forth with peace. (Isaiah 55:12 NASB)

The apostle Paul uses interesting language to describe the role of peace in our lives:

> Let the peace of Christ rule in your hearts. (Colossians 3:15)

The word "rule" in this passage is the Greek word *brabeuo*, which means "to be an umpire." Like a baseball umpire, the peace of God announces whether you're "safe" in God's will, or "out" of God's will.

When we receive the greatest miracle there could ever be by accepting Jesus Christ as our Savior, God's presence is so palpable, we're literally basking in his peace. We know that we know that we know we have discovered the meaning and reason for existence—to know God and to live with him forever!

D. **Man wonders if it is God communicating.**

In the process of trying to determine what is happening as the Holy Spirit begins speaking to your heart, you likely will go through a process of questioning.

- Are these just my own thoughts?
- Do I need to get my head examined?
- Who is speaking?
- Is this some unknown god?
- Are these aliens I'm hearing?
- Is this the devil speaking to me?

When the unseen spirit world collides with our untrained senses, it is natural to question the origin of the message. Our first encounters with God can be similar to the experience of the character Neo in the movie *The Matrix* when he is awakened to the real world. In the movie, machines have taken over the human race, hooking them up to a vast computer program called "the Matrix" while the machines live off the electrical impulses of the human bodies. The humans think their world is real, while all the time they are living out computer-generated pseudo-experiences created by the Matrix. The few who escape the Matrix discover the real world, which is called Zion.

Neo escapes into Zion, where he must relearn all he has learned in the false world of the Matrix.

Our salvation experience has many parallels to Neo's journey out of the Matrix. In our fallen state, we seem to be merrily living our lives seeking happiness and fulfillment. Like Neo, many reach a crisis in life where they wonder, "Is this all there is? There must be something more." Like the atheistic C. S. Lewis or the fictional Neo, they get a glimpse into the spirit realm and realize this is the greater reality. Panic sets in initially as everything that was once thought to be reality is turned on its head. But then we are flooded with peace and trust begins to slowly grow.

E. **God always calls us to a higher level.**

"I know the plans I have for you," declares our loving heavenly Father, "plans for welfare and not for evil, to give you a future and a hope" (Jeremiah 29:11). God's intention for us is not only for our good, but is meant to stretch us in ways that will allow us to reach levels in ourselves we could not imagine. He wants us to extend our faith to dream so audaciously only God could intervene to see it become a reality.

The psalmist declares:

> Blessed are those whose strength is in you, in whose heart are the highways to Zion. ... They go from **strength to strength**. (Psalm 84:5, 7, italics and emphasis added)

The writer of Proverbs explains:

> The path of the righteous is like the light of dawn, which shines **brighter and brighter until full day.** (Proverbs 4:18, italics and emphasis added)

In both our natural and spiritual lives, we are either moving forward or backward—there is no neutral. Those who pause on a plateau soon find themselves surpassed by others who keep their forward momentum.

In the natural world, this is called a paradigm shift. We saw a massive paradigm shift begin a quarter century ago when the world made the transition from analog to digital. That major paradigm shift is still reverberating. We've gone from vinyl LPs and cassette tapes to digital music players that hold thousands of songs. We've gone from televisions with antennas to smart TVs. The changes in the digital space continue to evolve and expand at lightning speed.

Laws in the spirit realm are just as real as our natural laws of gravity and thermodynamics. This includes what Pat Robertson calls "The Law of Use." In the natural world, body builders will begin lifting weights by doing a series of repetitions over several days. As their muscles grow, athletes add more weight to the barbell. It may be a struggle at first to lift the added weight, but again, over time muscles grow because of the ongoing repetition. Weights are continually added as they sculpt and shape their muscles. The moment they discontinue the repetitions, their muscles begin to shrink in size. "Use it or lose it," is an often-heard mantra of athletes.

In fact, if you strapped the arm of an athlete to restrict movement, over time it would atrophy, and eventually, they would not be able to lift it at all.

The "Law of Use" works the same way in the spirit/soul realm. As we exercise our faith, our spiritual gifts and talents grow and bear fruit. When we stop using the gifts, abilities, and faith God has given us, these things start to diminish. That is why God is always calling us to a higher level in him and in the kingdom.

We see this concept clearly stated in the parable of the talents.

> To one he gave five talents, to another two, to another one, to each according to his ability. ... He who had received the five talents went at once and traded with them, and he made five talents more. So also he who had the two talents made two talents more. But he who had received the one talent went and dug in the ground and hid his master's money.
>
> Now after a long time the master of those servants came and settled accounts with them. And he who had received the five talents came forward, bringing five talents more, saying, "Master, you delivered to me five talents; here, I have made five talents more." His master said to him, "Well done, good and faithful servant. You have been faithful over a little; I will set you over much. Enter into the joy of your master."
>
> He also who had received the one talent came forward, saying, "Master, I knew you to be a hard man, reaping where you did not sow, and gathering where you scattered no seed, so I was afraid, and I went and hid your talent in the ground. Here, you have what is yours." But his master answered him, "You wicked and slothful servant! ...Take the talent from him and give it to him who has the ten talents. For to everyone who has will more be given, and he will have an abundance. But from the one who has not, even what he has will be taken away." (Matthew 25:15–29)

This seems like a harsh teaching, but sometimes reality is just that. God wants us to be good stewards of the talents he has given us. It gives him great joy to see us extend our faith to reach the high calling he challenges us to reach—for his glory, for his kingdom, and for those we are called to reach with the message of God's love for them.

F. **We recognize the communication is from God, and we must decide whether to act on God's instruction.**

One of the distinguishing aspects of human beings is our ability to make a choice. Billy Graham explains, "When

God created you, He gave you the ability to make moral choices. And one of the choices that He gives you to make is what you're going to do about his Son, Jesus Christ."

Just as Peter, Paul, and Mary had to decide to obey the call of God in their lives, we too must decide to turn from our own sinful, selfish ways and turn our lives over to Jesus.

Another vital aspect of the decision made by Peter, Paul, and Mary was that their choice could lead to their natural death—and it would certainly lead to them dying to control over their own lives.

- Peter was a professional fisherman who had sailed the Sea of Galilee for decades. He knew the treacherous water during that storm could possibly lead to his death if Jesus didn't intervene. He was consciously risking his life by stepping onto the water.
- Saul and his compatriots were on a mission to harass, imprison, and possibly even murder the followers of Jesus. He knew if he suddenly had a change of heart, his fellow Pharisees could turn on him and possibly kill him.
- Mary knew if she was found to be pregnant without being married, she could be stoned. She also consciously risked her life by obeying the call of God.

By surrendering our lives to the lordship of Jesus Christ, we too are laying down our lives. To confess **the Lord Jesus Christ** is to give up control of our lives and to follow the Good Shepherd. That is what water baptism symbolizes. As we dunk under the water, we symbolically and spiritually die to our own plans and purposes. We emerge from the water, as Paul teaches, "a new creation; the old things passed away; behold, new things have come" (2 Corinthians 5:17 NASB).

G. **Once a decision is made there must be corresponding action, taking the experience from the spiritual into the natural realm.**

Peter had to lift his foot over the side of that boat before the miracle of walking on water could take place. Saul had to obey Jesus's instruction and go into Damascus to wait for further instructions. But Mary's action is most like our salvation experience. After Mary decided to obey the call of God to carry the Messiah in her womb, she spoke these kingdom-shaking words:

> Behold, I am the servant of the Lord; let it be to me according to your word. (Luke 1:38)

While Peter and Paul pulled the principle from spirit/soul into the natural realm with their physical actions, Mary did so with her words—through her confession of faith. Significantly, the apostle Paul explains that our salvation comes about by our confession of faith.

In the famous passage, Romans 10:9–10 (NASB), Paul describes the salvation experience. First, he writes in verse 9:

> If you **confess with your mouth** [natural realm] Jesus as Lord, and **believe in your heart** [spiritual realm] that God raised Him from the dead, you will be saved.

Then he reiterates this truth in Hebraic teaching style and further clarifies the spiritual event in verse 10:

> For **with the heart a person believes**, [spirit/soul realm] resulting in **righteousness**, and **with the mouth he confesses**, [natural realm] resulting in **salvation**.

This is an explicit example of how the miracle occurs in the Peter, Paul, and Mary principle after there is corresponding action. While belief has occurred in the heart leading to righteousness, it is not until confession is made with the mouth—transferring the process from the spirit to the natural realm—and then, Paul teaches that salvation occurs. After Mary's confession of faith with her mouth—the action bringing the process into the natural realm—was when the Holy Spirit overshadowed her, and she conceived. After we confess with our mouth—the process of praying the prayer and declaring that Jesus Christ is Lord—the action bringing the process into the natural realm—salvation occurs.

> H. **In faith, the action is taken, based on the instruction of the Lord. At that moment, the grace of God comes on the scene, mixing with the Word of God, the faith, and the action—in this case bringing about the miracle of salvation, and we become a new creation in Christ.**

Now that we have seen how the Peter, Paul, and Mary principle works in our salvation experience, let's examine how understanding this concept can unlock our faith even further. From this understanding, we can step into our birthright to receive from God all that is needed to live the abundant life Jesus offers to those who follow him.

—CHAPTER EIGHT
—FAITH FOR GUIDANCE

To experience abundant life, there are certain spiritual gifts or tools God has made available to us as followers of Jesus to help us on our journey. One of these is the promise of God's guidance. Like all heavenly gifts, God's guidance must be received by faith.

Going down the PP&M checklist, we see the pattern.

A. **Our loving heavenly Father desires to have a relationship with us and direct us toward his will, so he initiates the communication.**

B. **The possibility of being directed by Almighty God fills many with fear, confusion, and anxiety.**

C. **Jesus gives the comforting promise that "My sheep hear my voice." The Bible also tells us "the steps of the righteous person are ordered of the Lord" (Psalm 37:23). These and other biblical promises of God's direction bring God's peace.**

D. **Learning to discern the voice of God from the other possible voices we can hear makes us wonder if it is really God communicating.**

E. **God calls us to a higher level of our walk with him by revealing his will to us through the communication of the Holy Spirit.**

F. Through trial and error, we learn to recognize the voice of God, and then we must decide whether to act on God's direction.

G. Once a decision is made, we must act in a corresponding manner, that is, following God's direction in a tangible way. This action moves the experience from the spiritual into the natural realm.

H. In faith, we act, the grace of God comes on the scene, mixing with the direction of God and he moves in our life to accomplish his purpose.

MAKING THE RIGHT CHOICES

Every person has at one time wondered if they are making the right choices in life. For the believer, it is the cry of the heart to do what is pleasing for our heavenly Father. God wants to reveal himself and to communicate with us. But it's not always easy for us to know we are actually hearing his voice.

Yet Jesus promised we would literally hear his voice. Speaking of himself as the Good Shepherd, he declared:

> The sheep follow him, for they know his voice. A stranger they will not follow, but they will flee from him, for they do not know the voice of strangers. (John 10:4–5)

God has revealed in Scripture certain key ways in which he typically communicates with people. We can grow in confidence to know God speaking to our heart is just as normal as one person talking to another. What kind of a heavenly Father would he be if he created us, but chose not to communicate? The key to unlocking the door to hearing from God is to take the step of faith by incrementally acting on the direction you are sensing from heaven.

DILIGENTLY SEEKING GOD'S WILL

When we're diligent in our pursuit of God and in our desire to know his will, he will allow opportunities for us to learn how to discern his voice. When we pray, "Heavenly Father, make clear to me what your will is in this choice you have set before me," God will answer your prayer. But he will likely do so in a manner that forces us to engage in an analysis of what I call the seven keys of God's guidance:

- The Scriptures,
- The Holy Spirit speaking directly to your spirit,
- Godly counsel of mature Christian leaders,
- Peace or lack of peace in your spirit,
- Personal prophecy,
- Confirmation through multiple sources, and
- The circumstances surrounding the decision.

As we step out in faith to hear God's voice, we may have an impression, or a strong sense of peace a certain course of action is from God. We may receive advice from a pastor, friend, mentor, or a trusted family member that helps point us in a certain direction. Circumstances may arise that give us a clear indication our choice is either a good or a bad one. The door may even close altogether. But in this process of trial and error we're learning—and if we're diligent, in time we'll begin to recognize God's voice and distinguish it from the others.

However, the leading comes, we must act based on what we believe God is speaking in order to move from the spiritual to the natural. Once this step of faith has been taken, we wait to see what happens. It may turn out to be a wonderful decision, with an unmistakable outpouring of God's blessing. Or it could be there is no immediate outward indication that is either positive or negative. If so, press on until time makes clear whether this choice was or was not of God. Then again, you may experience some negative consequences because of your choice, making it clear God's leading was missed—and that's okay. In all of this you're learning to hear and discern the voice of your heavenly Father.

SAMUEL GROWS IN FAITH TO HEAR GOD

A person just learning to hear the voice of God is like the boy Samuel in the Old Testament. The Bible tells us Samuel served in the temple under the high priest, Eli. This was a time of corruption in Israel, and Scripture tells us that "The word of the Lord was rare in those days; there was no frequent vision" (1 Samuel 3:1). Then Samuel's first lesson in hearing the voice of God began to unfold.

Samuel did not yet know the Lord, and the word of the Lord had not yet been revealed to him. One night, the Lord called Samuel as he slept. The boy rose and answered, "Here I am!" Acting on what he thought was his master's voice, he ran to Eli and said, "Here I am, for you called me." Awakened in the middle of the night, Eli answered with a prickly response: "I did not call; lie down again." Confused, the boy went back to his bed and lay down.

A short time later the Lord called again, "Samuel!" Once again, the boy arose and went to Eli. "Here I am, for you called me." Annoyed by another disturbance to his sleep, Eli shot back, "I did not call, my son; lie down again."

The Lord called Samuel again the third time. He once again arose and went to Eli, saying, "Here I am, for you called me." Then Eli perceived the Lord was calling the boy. Eli said to Samuel, "Go, lie down, and if he calls you, you shall say, 'Speak, LORD, for your servant hears.'" (1 Samuel 3:4-9)

You see, Samuel could not yet discern between the voice of God and the voice of his master, Eli. In time, Samuel would grow to recognize God's voice so well he became one of the greatest prophets in the history of Israel.

Like Samuel, we can learn to discern the voice of God speaking to our hearts. Through the seven keys, every possible leading can be weighed to tell whether it is a message from God, our flesh, the world, or from Satan. These keys are like a divine checklist when considering His guidance.

God does speak today, and we can hear his voice. But we must be careful—especially as a young Christian—to seek ways to objectively confirm we are following the Holy Spirit and not another voice. Our own flesh can scream pretty loud, especially when we're under pressure, or we want something very badly. The world can also be seductive. And the devil is the father of lies—he is the great deceiver.

But God has provided a road map to help guide us into his plan for our lives.

The Seven Keys—An Overview

Let's look more closely at these seven basic keys or filters.

1. **Scripture**

Every possible leading, every dream, every piece of advice from a godly friend, every prophetic word, every voice we hear or sermon from the pulpit must line up with God's Word. The Bible must be the first and foremost plumb line for all we do in life. Paul gives this exhortation:

> All Scripture is breathed out by God, and is profitable for teaching, for reproof, for correction, for training in righteousness, that the man of God may be complete, equipped for every good work. (2 Timothy 3:16–17)

God will never contradict Scripture. This is a great assurance as we seek his guidance. And we only know what is truly right and wrong based on God's revelation to us from the Scripture.

2. **The Holy Spirit speaking to our heart**

As we have already seen, God speaks to his children, and we can hear his voice, which is part of the covenant we have with God as New Testament believers.

> "I will put my laws into their minds, and will write them upon their hearts. And I will be their God, and they shall be my people. And they shall not teach, each one his fellow citizen, and each one his brother, saying, 'know the Lord,' for all shall know Me, from the least to the greatest of them." (Hebrews 8:10–11 NASB)

We can't be led only by what we perceive to be the voice of God. We must balance any potential guidance with the other six keys. But rest assured, if you are truly seeking Almighty God—the God of the Bible—and are humble in your heart, you will learn to discern His voice and he will direct your steps.

3. **Godly counsel**

Where there is no guidance, a people falls, but in an abundance of counselors there is safety. (Proverbs 11:14)

We need each other. No one can fully comprehend the leading of God on their own because we all have blind spots and weaknesses. These are the places where we are vulnerable to deception. As we walk together with other believers, we can receive counsel and direction from one another that comes from the Spirit of God. The apostle Paul speaks of this in his letter to the church in Corinth:

> To each is given the manifestation of the Spirit for the common good. ... As it is, there are many parts, yet one body. The eye cannot say to the hand, "I have no need of you," nor again the head to the feet, I have no need of you." (1 Corinthians 12:7, 20–21)

We need to be humble and willing to receive and prayerfully consider input from those leaders that God places in our lives. The writer of Hebrews encourages us to:

> Remember those who led you, who spoke the word of God to you; and considering the result of their conduct, imitate their faith. (Hebrews 13:7 NASB)

And

> Obey your leaders and submit to them—for they keep watch over your souls as those who will give an account. (Heb. 13:17 NASB)

In addition to seeking to hear the voice of the Holy Spirit in prayer, we should also seek to hear him through the godly leaders in our lives. Jesus will speak through pastors and mentors placed in our lives. These are people of faith with whom we have a trusting relationship. It's not wise to open the circle of our most intimate friendships too wide—but neither is it spiritually healthy to keep all things about our walk with the Lord to ourselves. We should seek mature men and women of God who will act as sounding boards for the direction we believe we're hearing from the Lord.

4. **The peace of God**

> Let the peace of Christ rule in your hearts, to which indeed you were called in one body. And be thankful. (Colossians 3:15)

One way to avoid missing God's direction is to check what I call our "peace-ometer." God's peace helps us to know his leading in our lives when we are considering a decision.

5. **Personal prophecy (word of knowledge, word of wisdom)**

Prophecy can be defined simply as God communicating his thoughts and desires to man through other people. Dr.

Bill Hamon, a respected prophetic leader, gives this caution about the prophetic: "Though personal prophecy can play an important role in helping Christians make decisions, it is by no means the only way the Holy Spirit uses to reveal God's will and way. Probably 90 percent of my decisions, major and minor, have been made without personal prophecy being the dominating or even motivating faction. But I have striven to make 100 percent of all my decisions based upon God's Word, will, and way."[1]

The Bible clearly tells us to be receptive to prophetic words:

> Do not quench the Spirit. Do not despise prophecies. (1 Thessalonians 5:19–20)

But the very next verse tells us to be cautious in our approach to the prophetic:

> But test everything; hold fast to what is good. (verse 21)

6. **Confirmation**

> So that on the testimony of two or three witnesses every matter may be confirmed. (Matthew 18:16 NASB)

Confirmation is reassurance we have heard from God and are on the right track in following his guidance. Confirmation can come in a thousand different ways—it's up to the Lord which way he chooses. These confirmations are often the most dramatic and faith-confirming aspects of our Christian walk. Often the other six keys provide confirmation of God's direction.

7. **Circumstances/Timing**

Circumstances should not be ignored or magnified when seeking the will of God in our lives. Many Christians are on either end of the spectrum regarding their view of circumstances and God's guidance. Some less mature Christians are led entirely by circumstances and completely ignore the other six keys. Then there are those "spooky spiritual" believers who completely ignore the circumstances of life because they claim to have heard the voice of God. They don't check this guidance against the other six keys. If we will properly weigh circumstances—including God's timing—along with the other keys of God's guidance, we will see God bring tremendous spiritual fruit to our lives.

The Lord will direct the circumstances of our lives to move us here and there as he desires. He will also plant his desires in our hearts. We may think it is merely our own good idea. When we get to heaven, I think we're going to be amazed at how often the Lord directed our steps when we weren't even aware of it.

As we humble ourselves before the Lord and seek his guidance in our lives, the Good Shepherd will be faithful to lead us, "in paths of righteousness for his name's sake" (Psalm 23:3).

Now that we know that God desires to guide our steps, let's examine the fact that he also wants to provide the things we need.

—CHAPTER NINE—
FAITH FOR PROVISION

The pursuit of provision is something we all face every day of our lives. For some, the acquisition of wealth is looked upon as the measure of success. In certain parts of the world, however, just having what is needed for daily life is considered wealth. For most people, provision—to have one's basic needs met—is part of an abundant life. God promises that he will meet our needs, but when times are difficult or we are facing a looming deadline, provision must be received by faith.

Let's review the PP&M checklist to see the pattern.

A. Our loving heavenly Father has initiated the communication by promising to provide for our every need.

B. Despite this promise, many are filled with the fear that somehow God will not fulfill his Word—even though it is an explicit promise in the Bible.

C. The words of Jesus from the Sermon on the Mount are comforting: "So if you sinful people know how to give good gifts to your children, how much more will your heavenly Father give good gifts to those who ask him" (Matthew 7:11 NLT). Along with many other biblical promises of God's provision, this brings God's peace.

D. When times get tight or deadlines loom, we can sometimes wonder if God has really promised to provide for our needs.

E. God calls us to the higher level of believing he will provide, despite the looming circumstances.

F. We must decide to trust God and not to worry.

G. Once we've decided to trust and not worry, we must act in agreement with that decision and take the experience from the spiritual into the natural realm.

H. In faith, action is taken, the grace of God comes on the scene, mixing with the promise of provision and he moves to meet our needs—and sometimes, to give us the desires of our hearts.

WHAT GOD'S WORD SAYS ABOUT PROVISION

I remember when I was in graduate school with three children all under the age of six. I had moved from Pennsylvania to Virginia to further my education. At the time, I had difficulty finding a job that I could work around my class schedule. The first few months were quite challenging as I attended classes, completed my homework, and then worked a night job to help meet the needs. In addition to the challenge of tuition, books, and other school-related expenses, we faced the difficulty of finding childcare. During this stressful time of transition, it was difficult to maintain my faith in God's promise to provide.

In those first lean months of graduate school, the Holy Spirit continually reminded me of the words of Jesus from the Sermon on the Mount.

> Therefore I tell you, do not be anxious about your life, what you will eat or what you will drink, nor about your

body, what you will put on. Is not life more than food, and the body more than clothing? Look at the birds of the air: they neither sow nor reap nor gather into barns, and yet your heavenly Father feeds them. Are you not of more value than they? (Matthew 6:25–26 ESV)

I must admit, I was having a hard time with this passage. At the moment, it seemed God was not holding up his end of the bargain. We were struggling to make ends meet. Yet I had seen God provide for my family again and again since childhood, so I *decided* to doubt my fears and to trust the promises of God. I began to read through his promises of provision and to thank him for being faithful to his Word. I read the rest of Jesus teaching from the Sermon on the Mount.

But if God so clothes the grass of the field, which today is alive and tomorrow is thrown into the oven, will he not much more clothe you, O you of little faith? Therefore do not be anxious, saying, "What shall we eat?" or "What shall we drink?" or "What shall we wear?" For the Gentiles seek after all these things, and your heavenly Father knows that you need them all. But seek first the kingdom of God and his righteousness, and all these things will be added to you. (Matthew 6:30–33)

Despite my anxious feelings, I stood firm on the promises of God and continued to thank him for making a way where there seemed to be no way. Within a few weeks, the door opened for me to be the painter of the student housing apartment complex. This was a full-time job providing pay, health benefits, the flexibility to attend classes as needed during the day, and help with tuition. God had answered my prayers by providing literally everything I needed.

BIBLICAL PROMISES ON PROVISION

Throughout Scripture, we find multiple verses where God promises to be our provider. In the book of Genesis, we learn what is called the redemptive name of God regarding provision, "Yahweh Yireh," known also as "Jehovah Jireh," which means "the Lord will provide," after God provided for Abraham and Isaac a ram in the thicket to be used for their sacrifice.

> Abraham named the place Yahweh-Yireh (which means "the Lord will provide"). To this day, people still use that name as a proverb: "On the mountain of the Lord it will be provided." (Genesis 22:14 NLT)

Here are a few key promises of God's provision:

> My God will supply every need of yours according to his riches in glory in Christ Jesus. (Philippians 4:19)

> Every moving thing that lives shall be food for you. And as I gave you the green plants, I give you everything. (Genesis 9:3)

> Consider the ravens: they neither sow nor reap, they have neither storehouse nor barn, and yet God feeds them. Of how much more value are you than the birds! (Luke 12:24)

> Let us then with confidence draw near to the throne of grace, that we may receive mercy and find grace to help in time of need. (Hebrews 4:16)

> For the Lord God is a sun and shield; the Lord bestows favor and honor. No good thing does he withhold from those who walk uprightly. (Psalm 84:11)

> If you abide in me, and my words abide in you, ask whatever you wish, and it will be done for you. (John 15:7)

If you struggle with seeing God as your provider, you may want to commit these verses to memory to plant them deep in your heart—remembering faith comes by hearing the Word of God.

Acting in Faith: Doing Our Part

When it comes to receiving provision from God, people tend to fall somewhere along the spectrum of the two extremes. On the one hand, there are people who sit idly by and expect God to do everything. Then, they complain their needs are not met. We must remember this walk with God is a partnership. As we see in the parable of the talents, God provides us with what we need to begin—the ability, the intelligence, the ideas, and the energy—but we must go out and use what God has given us to multiply those gifts.

When I worked at CBN, Pat Robertson often shared what became known as "the cantaloupe and cottage cheese story." Years ago, Pat was at a conference in Anaheim, California, and one morning as he bowed his head to pray over his breakfast of cantaloupe and cottage cheese, the Lord spoke to his heart and said, "Build a university to my glory." As Pat shared this story in chapel, he explained what happened next. "Now I didn't go home, sit on the porch in a rocking chair, and wonder when God would provide the university. I went home and got to work. First, I did research on the legal requirements, then I started meeting with experts. We looked at possible locations and started doing interviews with professors. Soon, in partnership with our efforts, God raised up Regent University."

Once again, we must never forget everything we receive from God includes an element of action on our part.

On the other hand, some of us can go to the other extreme of working so hard we strain relationships with our spouses and our children, and even endanger our own health. I've seen many who say they are working for the Lord who end up divorced and estranged from their family because their priorities were not in proper order.

There can be many different motives driving overwork—fear, pride, greed, rejection. Sometimes, there's no choice as the circumstances of life force us to work to meet the pressing needs. I knew a professor once who also served as a pastor and advisor for a growing megachurch. I asked him why he worked so much, and he was remarkably honest in his reply. He had grown up in a lower middle-class family that always struggled to have enough. He vowed his wife and children would not have the same struggles. We then had a conversation about work-life balance, and we both determined there is no easy answer for where the line is drawn. Overwork can be a lack of faith in God's promise to provide. Only the Holy Spirit can tell us if we step over from faith to fear and are working beyond what is best for us and our family.

Working for the Lord and to provide for our family can be a joy as long as it is balanced with enjoying life and the precious people he places around you.

How Many Forests?

The God of the Bible is a God of abundance. In God's economy, we don't ask how many acorns are in the forest, but instead, how many forests are in the acorn. The Bible declares, "While the earth remains, seedtime and harvest ... shall not cease" (Genesis 8:22). Planting seeds and reaping a harvest happens in both the natural and the spiritual realms—and in both there is an element of faith, corresponding action, and a time of waiting for the harvest.

Jesus taught this important concept regarding giving and receiving:

> Give, and it will be given to you. They will pour into your lap a good measure—pressed down, shaken together, and running over. For by your standard of measure it will be measured to you in return. (Luke 6:38 NASB)

This process is also known by the agricultural metaphor of sowing and reaping. If we plant one corn seed in good soil, then water it and keep the weeds away, over time that plant will emerge first as the blade of a green sprout. Soon the stalk begins to form and then ears of corn will emerge.

In the fullness of time, the ears of corn would be filled with hundreds and maybe thousands of individual corn seeds.

The same occurs in the kingdom of God. Jesus is using another agricultural metaphor here to describe the process of spiritual sowing and reaping. He says, "give and it will be given to you." That gift could be of money, of talent, of time, of material possession—whatever we believe God is calling us to give. Then, Jesus describes how our gift will be multiplied, just like that corn seed—"pressed down, shaken together, and running over."

Jesus goes on to explain how our harvest is related to the motive and nature of our heart as we give. "For by your standard of measure it will be measured to you in return." The apostle Paul explained this way: "The point is this: whoever sows sparingly will also reap sparingly, and whoever sows bountifully will also reap bountifully" (2 Corinthians 9:6).

In the same letter to the Corinthians, Paul reminds them of the importance of giving as part of the life of a disciple of Jesus:

> Since you excel in so many ways—in your faith, your gifted speakers, your knowledge, your enthusiasm, and your love from us—I want you to excel also in this gracious act of giving. (2 Corinthians 8:7 NLT)

The Good News Translation uses this practical language: "Remember that the person who plants few seeds will have a small crop; the one who plants many seeds will have a large crop." (2 Corinthians 9:6 GNT)

The prophet Malachi challenges us with this promise from God:

> Bring the full tithe into the storehouse, that there may be food in my house. And thereby put me to the test, says the Lord of hosts, if I will not open the windows of

> heaven for you and pour down for you a blessing until there is no more need. I will rebuke the devourer for you, so that it will not destroy the fruits of your soil, and your vine in the field shall not fail to bear, says the Lord of hosts. (Malachi 3:10–11)

It's important for us to remember everything belongs to God, and we are merely caretakers of the things he entrusts to us. Jesus reminds us we are stewards in the Gospel of Luke.

> One who is faithful in a very little is also faithful in much, and one who is dishonest in a very little is also dishonest in much. If then you have not been faithful in the unrighteous wealth, who will entrust to you the true riches? (Luke 16:10–11)

One of the best Scriptures to memorize to help grow your faith for God's provision is Proverbs 3:5–6 and 9–10 (NLT):

> Trust in the Lord with all your heart; do not depend on your own understanding. Seek his will in all you do, and he will show you which path to take. ... Honor the LORD with your wealth and with the best part of everything you produce. Then he will fill your barns with grain, and your vats will overflow with good wine.

As we grow in our trust in the Lord for provision, we can now examine God's promise to bring healing in our physical bodies.

—CHAPTER TEN—
FAITH FOR HEALING

After I served as a full-time hospital chaplain for two years, the lesson was reinforced again and again that God's promise of healing is dealt out to us according to his plan for our lives and not according to our preconceived theology. Health and healing for what we may call a normal person is a dream for someone with a genetic disorder or a chronic disease. It's important to remember everyone Jesus healed during his earthly ministry ultimately died. Health and healing on planet earth during this parenthesis in eternity called time is a fleeting thing.

We can and should believe God for healing in our lives, but we should also realize in this fallen and corrupted world, health will come to different people in different ways. Like every gift from God, healing is received by faith. Our job is to believe God loves us and his biblical promises are ultimately true. God then provides health and healing to us as he sees fit—with ultimate healing coming in heaven or when Jesus returns.

Let's review the PP&M checklist to see the pattern of receiving healing in our lives.

    A. Our loving Heavenly Father has initiated the communication by promising healing in the Bible.

B. Despite this promise, many are filled with the fear and anxiety when a health crisis hits—or if they are facing chronic or genetic health issues in their lives.

C. The words of Jesus to many of those he healed during his time on earth bring comfort and peace to those struggling with their health today. Jesus first makes the statement, "Your faith has made you well" when he heals the woman with the issue of blood (Matthew 9:22). He tells her to "go in peace" (Mark 5:34). Jesus also says, "Your faith has made you well," to a blind beggar (Luke 18:42), the ten lepers (Luke 17:19), and others.

D. When enduring pain, facing medical procedures, fighting mounting healthcare bills, recovering from surgery, or just enduring a chronic illness, we can sometimes wonder if God has really promised to provide healing to our bodies in this world.

E. God calls us to the higher level of faith and healing amid the health challenges we face.

F. We must decide to trust God and not to worry.

G. Once we've decided, we must take a corresponding action to take the experience from the spiritual into the natural realm. One of the most important actions we can take is to guard the words of our mouths. In addition to believing the biblical promises regarding healing, it is important for us to verbally declare these promises are for us—this is a way to bring the promise from the spiritual to the natural realm as we put action to our faith.

H. When we respond in faith and then act upon the promise of God, the grace of God comes on the scene, and he brings healing into our lives. Sometimes this healing is incremental. Sometimes it is a lifting of pain. Sometimes it is healing for a time. Then there are times where God does a miracle, bringing total and complete healing. In all these things we give thanks to our loving heavenly Father for his love, mercy, and grace.

WHAT GOD'S WORD SAYS ABOUT HEALING

The Bible is quite explicit in declaring that healing is a part of our covenant with God. The psalmist declares:

> He sent out his **word** and **healed them**, snatching them from the door of death. (Psalm 107:20 NLT, italics and emphasis added)

The apostle John uses the term "word" in the first chapter of his gospel:

> The Word became flesh and dwelt among us, and we have seen his glory. (John 1:14)

I believe these two verses are tied together in the commonality of "the Word." John is coupling Jesus to God's Word—and it is "the Word" that was sent forth that brought healing. Isaiah prophesied about the suffering Servant, declaring of him:

> But he was pierced for our transgressions; he was crushed for our iniquities; upon him was the chastisement that brought us peace, and with his wounds we are healed. (Isaiah 53:5)

Peter witnessed the suffering of Jesus, perhaps seeing with his own eyes Jesus being whipped as he faced crucifixion. He witnessed the risen Christ with wounds in his hands, feet, and side. Having seen with his eyes the completed work of Jesus, it is significant Peter uses the past tense to quote from Isaiah when he writes, "By his wounds you have been healed" (1 Peter 2:24).

The apostle James writes concerning healing:

> Are any of you sick? You should call for the elders of the church to come and pray over you, anointing you with oil in the name of the Lord. Such a prayer offered in faith will heal the sick, and the Lord will make you well. (James 5:14–15 NLT)

King David proclaims:

> Bless the Lord, O my soul, and do not forget any of His benefits; Who pardons all your guilt, Who heals all your diseases. (Psalm 103:2–3 NASB)

Matthew observed the earthly ministry of Jesus, declaring:

> Jesus was going about in all of Galilee, teaching in their synagogues and proclaiming the gospel of the kingdom, and healing every disease and every sickness among the people. (Matthew 4:23 NASB)

There are many other Scriptures dealing with healing and wholeness in body and mind. Clearly healing is a biblical concept and a gift God wants for his children.

THE "WHY" QUESTION

At times, when believers face a chronic disease, a debilitating accident, or a sudden illness, many will cry out, "Why has God done this to me?" This question was posed to me as a hospital chaplain by an angry woman lying in a hospital bed.

"I'm only in my late 50s," she continued, "but I'm stuck in a body that's getting weaker and weaker. While my friends are out having fun and enjoying their lives, I'm trapped in this body and in this bed."

There are many ways I could have responded. I could have told her to "cheer up" and stop complaining. I could have told her "God works in mysterious ways." I could have told her that she could get better if she only had enough faith. Or I could have told her everything was going to be okay.

None of those are good responses. The best response was to listen and allow her to pour out her heart of pain.

After she was done, I simply acknowledged her pain and said I was sorry she had such a difficult burden to bear. I assured her of God's love for her, despite the health challenges she was facing.

As we continued to talk, I reminded her there were many people in the Bible who experienced different kinds of pain—some physical, some emotional—and they also brought their sorrow, grief, and questions to God. I shared how David often cried out to God in the Psalms. I assured her God didn't mind her sharing truthfully from her heart.

After nearly an hour of sharing, she ended our conversation with, "Thank you, I needed to share that. Despite my pain, I still believe." We prayed together, and I said goodbye.

Two days later, I received an emergency message on my pager asking me to return to this woman's room. She was actively dying, and she had no family or friends with her.

By the time I arrived in her room, she had already fallen into a coma, and the death struggle had begun. The nurse was getting ready to give her some morphine to ease her pain.

I took hold of the woman's hand and spoke to her, "It's Chaplain Craig. I was here a couple days ago. I want you to know you're not alone. I'm here, the nurse is here, and God is here with us."

I started to sing some hymns that were stirring in my heart. When I got to "Amazing Grace" the nurse said, "Oh, that is my favorite. Can I sing along?"

"Of course," I responded and the two of us sang the beloved hymn together. Then I started quoting what is probably the best known of David's writings—the 23rd Psalm.

When I spoke the comforting words, "Yea, though I walk through the valley of the shadow of death, I will fear no evil, for thou art with me …" this dear woman—who had not moved at all up until that point—suddenly squeezed my hand. I experienced then what I had had been told in my chaplain training, those in a coma can usually hear and understand what is happening around them.

Though she had questioned God during her difficult trial, she had held on to her faith. In the end, it was God's Word and his presence that brought her comfort as she said goodbye to this world.

The Bible gives us this comforting glimpse at God's perspective of earthly death:

> Precious in the sight of the Lord is the death of His godly ones. (Psalm 116:15 NASB)

I was honored to be there for this precious moment in the life of this godly one. And I was blessed to witness the power of God's Word to bring peace in the valley of the shadow of death. For this woman, healing was completed with her entry into the loving arms of Jesus.

On this earth, some walk in health throughout their lives, and some struggle with lifelong illness. Some have a mix of health and sickness at various times in their lives. God can and does bring healing to all of us at various times in our lives and in different ways—sometime in ways we may not realize or understand in this lifetime. As I have said, the ultimate healing will come to each one of us when we die and receive our new and glorified bodies in heaven—or when Jesus returns to rule as King of the earth. We can take comfort in the promise of ultimate healing from John's Revelation:

> Behold, the dwelling place of God is with man. He will dwell with them, and they will be his people, and God himself will be with them as their God. He will wipe

away every tear from their eyes, and death shall be no more, neither shall there be mourning, nor crying, nor pain anymore, for the former things have passed away. (Revelation 21:3–4)

—CHAPTER ELEVEN—
FAITH FOR FAVOR

During my chaplain residency, my supervisor made a remarkable statement: "Theology drives everything in life." I thought about this statement for a long time and concluded it is absolutely true. Our view of God—who he is. How we relate to him. Is he loving? Is he all-powerful and all-knowing? Has he revealed his will and his guidelines for how we live our lives? —all flows from our theological viewpoint.

Is God a personal, heavenly Father, or is he a deity who created the universe and then left it to its own devices? Or is there no such thing as a personal God, but only some cosmic force?

Is God's love freely given? Or does he require us to submit to a system of religious rules to obtain his favor?

Our lives and how we live them revolve around the answers to these theological questions.

How we see God changes how we see our world. But it is equally true that understanding how God sees us radically changes how we see ourselves.

Another way of approaching this question is through a concept commonly referred to as "knowing who we are in Christ."

One of the most revolutionary revelations I ever received was the understanding of who I am in Christ. I learned as believers we can see ourselves in two ways:

1. We can see ourselves as unworthy sinners who must constantly repent for our mistakes. In this scenario, God is an angry deity requiring constant humiliation and self-deprecation. In this view, salvation is unsure, as someone may die suddenly without having the chance to seek forgiveness from this task-master God for any unconfessed sin.

This worldview can be clearly seen in William Shakespeare's *Hamlet*. After Hamlet reveals through a play his uncle, the new king, has murdered Hamlet's father, the former king, the guilty uncle departs to a chapel to repent of his sins. Hamlet finds him there and is tempted to kill him yet withholds his hand—though not for a biblical reason.

"A villain kills my father," Hamlet debates aloud, "and, for that, I, his sole son, do this same villain send to heaven. Oh, this is hire and salary, not revenge. ... To take him in the purging of his soul when he is fit and seasoned for his passage? ... When he is drunk, asleep, or in his rage ... or about some act that has no relish of salvation in 't—Then trip him, that his heels may kick at heaven, and that his soul may be as damned and black as hell, whereto it goes."[1]

Using biblical language, Hamlet doesn't kill his murderous uncle because he is in the midst of "repentance"—which would risk him going to heaven. Instead, the prince plots to kill the king when he is sinning so he will go straight to hell. This is entertaining dialogue—but it's not New Testament gospel.

2. We can instead see ourselves, in the words of the New Testament: "Anyone who belongs to Christ has become a new person. The old life is gone; a new

life has begun!" (2 Corinthians 5:17 NLT) This is how your heavenly Father sees you once you receive Jesus as your Lord and Savior by faith. You're no longer just an old sinner.

You were just a sinner before you surrendered your life to Jesus, but now you are a child of God—your sins have been paid for by the sacrifice of Jesus on the cross. Instead of having a sin-consciousness, the Bible encourages us to see ourselves as a new creation—aware of our righteousness before God.

As a result of this spiritual transformation, you now have favor with God—meaning that as a born-again believer, you have certain promises from God because of what Jesus did at Calvary. So, what does it mean to be "in Christ," and how does that change the way we live our lives?

Living "In Christ"

Whenever God interacts with humankind, it is because of a covenant—this is a binding agreement in many ways like a contract. Even to this day, some legal documents still use the ancient word "covenant" to describe a binding contract. The first of these biblical agreements is known as the Edenic Covenant, where God made humans in his image and delegated authority for them to rule on earth in relationship with him.

When Adam and Eve disobeyed God and ate the forbidden fruit from the tree of the knowledge of good and evil, God gave them a promise of a Savior or Messiah to one day restore the broken relationship—this is called the Adamic Covenant.

God also made a covenant with Noah after the flood, promising to never destroy the earth again by water. God made an agreement with Abraham to begin the process of redeeming mankind to himself through the faith and obedience (sound familiar) of this righteous man. This covenant was renewed and confirmed through Abraham's son, Isaac, and his grandson, Jacob—who God renamed Israel.

This set God's redemptive plan in motion, but there were other covenants along the way. After delivering the descendants of Israel from slavery in Egypt, God gave his Law through Moses and then created the Sinaitic Covenant as an agreement with the children of Israel. After finding what he called "a man after my own heart," God made a covenant with King David, promising that one of his descendants would occupy the throne of Israel forever.

When God gave the Mosaic Law through the Sinaitic Covenant, he included a list of blessings for keeping the law and a list of curses for disobeying the law (see Deuteronomy 28). One of the stipulations promised the Jews the land of Canaan as their homeland as long as the people obeyed the commandments of the law. However, if they failed to obey God's law they would be expelled from the promised land.

From that point forward, God sent prophets to remind the people to keep up their side of the bargain and to obey the Mosaic Law. The problem was the children of Israel, who were part of the fallen race, were unable to keep the righteous requirements of the law. While there were many who tried to live according to the Law, even the best of them were unable to live up to the exacting standards of the Sinaitic Covenant. Even King David—the righteous warrior; the psalmist; the one who desired to build God's temple; the man after God's own heart—committed adultery with Bathsheba and then arranged to have her husband killed in battle.

Israel had some righteous rulers like King David and King Jehoshaphat, but most of them were disobedient—and even wicked. They turned their backs on God's law and even started worshipping the false gods of the surrounding nations. After multiple generations of rebellion, God finally sent one final prophet, Jeremiah, to warn them that their time in the promised Land was drawing to a close.

Now all of this may sound unjust of God, giving mankind righteous requirements they are unable to fulfill in their own strength and then tying their covenant and their remaining in their homeland to them keeping that law. It may seem unfair under the law of works—which is what every other religion on earth follows—but it makes complete sense under the new covenant God announced through Jeremiah. The prophet made this declaration just as King Nebuchadnezzar moved on Israel to defeat it and carry off the people into exile.

I've visited Israel and have driven down the steep ancient road from Jerusalem to Jericho. At one point, this road drops below sea level on its way to the lowest dry spot on earth at the Dead Sea. There are small cliffs in the mountains on each side of the road. I can imagine Jeremiah climbing up onto one of those cliffs as the mass of Jews are being driven to exile by the Babylonians below. Perhaps Jeremiah reminded them of the Sinaitic Covenant and that they would be expelled from the promised land for not obeying it. But then he may have shouted out this amazing promise of a new covenant that would come, bringing redemption to the children of Israel and to all the world:

> "Behold, the days are coming, declares the LORD, when I will make a new covenant with the house of Israel and the house of Judah, not like the covenant that I made with their fathers on the day when I took them by the hand to bring them out of the land of Egypt, my covenant that they broke, though I was their husband, declares the LORD. For this is the covenant that I will make with the house of Israel after those days, declares the LORD: I will put my law within them, and I will write it on their hearts. And I will be their God, and

they shall be my people. And no longer shall each one teach his neighbor and each his brother, saying, 'Know the LORD,' for they shall all know me, from the least of them to the greatest, declares the LORD. For I will forgive their iniquity, and I will remember their sin no more." (Jeremiah 31:31–34 ESV)

How is this possible? The children of Israel already demonstrated that mankind is incapable of keeping God's law—in other words, salvation by good works is an impossibility. There is no way to make an unbreakable covenant with sinful humanity.

At the same time, God had already delegated authority to humans on the earth, so short of annihilating the whole human race and starting over, God would have to deal somehow with people to bring about reconciliation.

Remember, God is perfect. There cannot be anything imperfect in his presence. At the same time, God is love, and he desires relationship with his creation. The prophecy of Jeremiah is clear the people of Israel broke their covenant, but now God planned to introduce a new covenant.

The only way this could be an unbreakable covenant is to make it between a holy God and a sinless person. This could only be done if God became human, living on earth with all the accompanying temptations and weaknesses of a man—yet empowered by the Holy Spirit to live without sin. This indescribable act of celestial love on God's part is known as the incarnation. And so ...

> The Word became flesh and dwelt among us, and we have seen his glory, glory as of the only Son from the Father, full of grace and truth. (John 1:14)
>
> For this is how God loved the world: He gave his one and only Son, so that everyone who believes in him will not perish but have eternal life. (John 3:16 NLT)
> Christ Jesus came into the world to save sinners, among whom I am foremost. (1 Timothy 1:15 NASB)

> But when the fullness of time had come, God sent forth his Son, born of woman, born under the law, to redeem those who were under the law, so that we might receive adoption as sons. (Galatians 4:4–5)
>
> And being found in human form, he humbled himself by becoming obedient to the point of death, even death on a cross. (Philippians 2:8)

A poem written by Pastor Frederick William Pitt (1859-1943) called "The Maker of the Universe" captures the amazing wonder of the incarnation of Christ. I first heard this poem in a song by the same name by the incomparable guitarist and vocalist Phil Keaggy.

> The maker of the universe, as man for man was made a curse:
> The claims of laws which He had made, unto the uttermost He paid.
> His holy fingers made the bough which grew the thorns that crowned His brow:
> The nails that pierced His feet were mined in secret places He designed.
> He made the forests where there sprung, the tree on which His body hung:
> He died upon a cross of wood, yet made the hill on which it stood.
> The sky that darkened o'er His head, by Him above the earth was spread:
> The sun that hid from Him his face, by His decree was poised in space.
> The spear revealing precious blood was tempered in the fires of God:
> The grave in which His form was laid, was hewn in rock which He had made.
> The throne on which He now appears was His from everlasting years:
> But a new glory crowns His brow, and every knee to Him must bow.[3]

So, because of the incarnation, God made a new and unbreakable covenant with humanity—sealed "in Christ" with Jesus representing the Trinity as the Son of God (Matthew 16:16–17) and Jesus representing humankind as the Son of Man (Matthew 9:6). Since he was fully man, Jesus was qualified to take upon himself the sins of humanity. Because he was fully God, he was able to live a sinless life. Jesus became "the Lamb of God who takes away the sins of the world," (John 1:29) just as John the Baptist proclaimed.

"That's great!" you may be thinking, "but what does it have to do with me?" The answer is

EVERYTHING!

Paul explained the problem to the Romans: "For everyone has sinned; we all fall short of God's glorious standard" (Romans 3:23 NLT). A few chapters later he expands on the problem, and then gives the solution: "For the wages of sin is death, but the free gift of God is eternal life through Christ Jesus our Lord." (Romans 6:23 NLT)

Eternal life comes by being "in Christ"—and this happens "by faith." We have no hope of salvation in ourselves, but if we receive the gift by receiving Jesus as the substitution for our sin, then our holy heavenly Father sees us as being in the covenant made between the Son of God and the Son of Man. When the Father looks at Jesus, he sees him as sinless. If you are "in Christ" by faith, the Father no long sees your sin or the mistakes of your past—he sees you as righteous.

This is why Paul declared, "For our sake he made **him to be sin who knew no sin**, so that IN HIM we might become the ***righteousness of God*** (2 Corinthians 5:21 ESV, italics and emphasis added).

As if this news isn't exciting enough, this life "in Christ" doesn't have to wait until we get to heaven. This abundant life "in Christ" begins the moment we receive Jesus as our Lord and Savior.

ALL PROMISES ARE YES

The apostle Paul makes this remarkable statement: "For as many as the promises of God are, ***in Him*** they are yes; therefore through Him also is our *Amen* to the glory of God through us." (2 Cor. 1:20 NASB, italics and emphasis added).

This passage gives us the assurance that all the promises the Bible makes to the people of God can be claimed by the followers of Jesus Christ. With confidence you can believe for and receive these biblical promises and more—like these:

> Little children, you are from God and have overcome them, for he who is in you is greater than he who is in the world. (1 John 4:4 ESV)
>
> No weapon that is fashioned against you shall succeed, and you shall refute every tongue that rises against you in judgment. This is the heritage of the servants of the Lord and their vindication is from me, declares the Lord. (Isaiah 54:17)
>
> Heal me, O Lord, and I shall be healed; save me, and I shall be saved, for you are my praise. (Jeremiah 17:14)
>
> And this same God who takes care of me will supply all your needs from his glorious riches, which have been given to us in Christ Jesus. (Philippians 4:19 NLT)
>
> The Lord is my shepherd, I shall not want. (Psalm 23:1 NASB)
>
> And God will generously provide all you need. Then you will always have everything you need and plenty left over to share with others. (2 Corinthians 9:8 NLT)
>
> Now all glory to God, who is able, through his mighty power at work within us, to accomplish infinitely more than we might ask or think. (Ephesians 3:20 NLT)

If you want to have some fun in your Bible study, do a search for the words "in him" or "in Christ" in the New Testament. You will be amazed by the promises that are yours because you are a part of this unbreakable new covenant by faith. One of the most remarkable chapters for finding passages using the words "in Christ" is Ephesians chapter 1. In just this one chapter, the apostle Paul uses the words "in Christ" or "in him" in verses 1, 3, 4, 7, 9, 10, 12, 13, 15, and 20.

Paul quotes the ancient poets when he declares in the book of Acts:

> 'In him we live and move and have our being'; as even some of your own poets have said, "'For we are indeed his offspring.'" (Acts 17:28)

Regarding this passage, *Meyers Commentary* observes: "Paul views God under the point of view of His immanence as the element in which we live, etc.; and man in such intimate connection with God, that he is constantly surrounded by the Godhead and embraced in its essential influence, but, apart from the Godhead, could neither live, nor move, nor exist."[2]

The psalmist declares God gives favor to the righteous—or those who are "in Christ:

> For You bless **the righteous** person, LORD. You **surround him with favor** as with a shield. (Psalm 5:12 NASB, italics and emphasis added)

In light of this amazing promise, let's review the PP&M checklist to see the pattern.

A. Our loving heavenly Father has initiated the communication by promising favor to the righteous in Christ.

B. Living in this fallen world where we make mistakes and sometimes fall back into sin, many of us are filled with the fear that somehow God will be so angry with us that he will not fulfill his promise.

C. The words of Paul and Peter are comforting:

> Therefore, since we have been justified by faith [we are 'in Christ'], we have peace with God through our Lord Jesus Christ. (Romans 5:1)

> May grace [favor] and peace be multiplied to you in the knowledge of God and of Jesus our Lord. (2 Peter 1:2)

Along with many other biblical promises of God's grace and favor, these passages bring his peace.

D. When times get tight or deadlines loom, we can sometimes wonder if God has really promised grace and favor in our time of need.

E. God calls us to the higher level of believing we are his children because of the sacrifice of Jesus on Calvary. He will provide, despite the looming circumstances.

F. We must decide to trust in God's love and favor and not to worry.

G. Once we've made that decision, we need respond with the appropriate action to take the experience from the spiritual into the natural realm.

H. In faith, the action is taken, the grace of God comes on the scene, mixing with the promise of favor and he moves to meet our needs.

It is appropriate to close this chapter with God's promise from the book of Hebrews:

> [Because we are in Christ], Let us then with confidence draw near to the ***throne of GRACE***, that we may receive mercy and ***find GRACE*** **[favor]** ***to help in time of need.*** (Hebrews 4:16, italics and emphasis added)

The Greek word for "grace" in this verse is *charis*, which is also translated "favor—that which affords joy, pleasure, delight, sweetness, charm, loveliness." Favor is your birthright—receive it by faith and walk in the abundant life Jesus has promised those who believe.

—CHAPTER TWELVE—
FAITH FOR THE GIFTS OF THE SPIRIT

> Pursue love, and earnestly desire the spiritual gifts, especially that you may prophesy. (1 Corinthians 14:1)

This one passage, written under the inspiration of the Holy Spirit by the apostle Paul, makes clear God's desire for the New Testament believer regarding how and why we are to allow the Holy Spirit to move through us to reach the world with the gospel. Let's break it down. God is love and he wants to show his love to his creation. One of the ways he does that is by speaking and moving through his people. The terms for this in the New Testament are used interchangeably—it is known both as "the manifestation of the Holy Spirit" and "the gifts of the Holy Spirit."

There are some theologians and pastors who teach that the gifts of the spirit were only for the early church and passed away with the death of the last apostle. This view is simply not biblical, not historical, and it does not line up with the powerful manifestations of the Holy Spirit in the earth today.

Other theologians teach that the gifts are for today, but you can only have one. They base this on Paul's response to the Corinthian church where he declares:

> For to one is given through the Spirit the utterance of wisdom, and to another the utterance of knowledge

according to the same Spirit, to another faith by the same Spirit, to another gifts of healing by the one Spirit, to another the working of miracles, to another prophecy, to another the ability to distinguish between spirits, to another various kinds of tongues, to another the interpretation of tongues. (1 Corinthians 12:8–10)

But this view is contrasted in the very next verse as Paul writes:

> All these are empowered by one and the same Spirit, **who apportions to each one individually as he wills**. (1 Corinthians 12:11, italics and emphasis added)

It is the Spirit of God who determines who receives what gifts. Why can I say this with confidence? Because in the first verse of chapter 14, Paul makes this statement:

> Pursue love, and **earnestly desire the spiritual gifts**, especially that you may *prophesy* (1 Corinthians 14:1, italics and emphasis added).

Here he distinguishes between two different manifestations of the Holy Spirit. First, he exhorts believers to "earnestly desire" (Greek *zeloo*, from which we get the English word zealous) the spiritual gifts (plural). Paul uses the Greek word *pneumatikos*, which means spiritual or spiritual things. Then he introduces a separate manifestation of the spirit when he adds "especially that you may prophesy." The word "especially" here is the Greek *mallon*, which means "all the more." The word "prophesy" is the Greek *propheteuo*, which means to foretell. Paul is distinguishing between his original mention of the spiritual gifts and this other manifestation of the spirit, the gift of prophecy.

The distinction is further cemented in subsequent verse 5 when he declares:

> Now I want you all to speak in tongues, but even more to prophesy.

This exhortation is a direct contradiction to the teaching that you only get one gift. How could Paul say in chapter 12 you only receive one gift of the Spirit, but then encourage people in this verse to operate in two?

In verse 6, Paul implies believers can move in multiple gifts when he asks the rhetorical question, "If I come to you speaking in tongues, how will I benefit you unless I bring you some revelation or knowledge or prophecy or teaching?"

In verse 13, Paul says clearly one person can pray for a subsequent gift: "Therefore, one who speaks in a tongue should pray that he may interpret."

In verse 31, Paul explains that every New Testament believer is able to prophesy under the leading of the Holy Spirit: "For you can all prophesy one by one, so that all may learn and all be encouraged." In the Greek, the literal translation is "you may (*dunamai*, meaning to be able) all (*pas*, meaning each of you) prophesy" (*propheteuo*, meaning to speak forth by divine inspiration). So, if everyone only has one gift, and everyone can prophesy, according to that logic, no one could move in any other gift—which, of course, contradicts Paul's teaching in chapter 12 about the various gifts that believers can manifest.

The truth is the manifestation of the gifts of the spirit are available for every believer to operate in by faith as needed. This is a wonderful part of our birthright.

God's Love in Tangible Ways

Theologians call the day of Pentecost the birthday of the church. On that day, a large group of Jesus's disciples were gathered in the upper room in Jerusalem in obedience to his instructions. Before ascending into heaven, Jesus told them to wait in Jerusalem until they were filled with power by the Holy Spirit (Acts 1:4–5). Then he told them why they were to wait:

> You will receive power when the Holy Spirit has come upon you, and you will be my witnesses in Jerusalem and in all Judea and Samaria, and to the end of the earth. (Acts 1:8)

When the day of Pentecost arrived, the disciples were united in prayer, and suddenly, the promised Holy Spirit fell upon them in power. They were all filled with the Holy Spirit and began speaking in other tongues—one of the gifts of the Spirit. As this supernatural event occurred during one of the key Jewish feasts, there were godly Jews "from every nation under heaven" gathered in Jerusalem for the observances. Luke paints a picture of the scene:

> At this sound the multitude came together, and they were bewildered, because each one was hearing them speak in his own language. And they were amazed and astonished, saying, "Are not all these who are speaking Galileans? And how is it that we hear, each of us in his own native language? ... We hear them telling in our own tongues the mighty works of God." And all were amazed and perplexed, saying to one another, "What does this mean?" But others mocking said, "They are filled with new wine." (Acts 2:6–13)

It seems the meeting spilled out from the upper room into the crowd gathered outside. Filled with exuberance at the infilling of the Holy Spirit, the disciples were bubbling over with praise for God. The amazing thing is the people who were gathered from various parts of the world were able to understand them. Theologians call this *glossolalia*, which is the phenomenon of speaking in an unknown language, especially in religious worship.

Bewildered, with some mocking the disciples as drunk, these pilgrims didn't know what to think. Led by the Holy Spirit, Peter stood and addressed the crowd:

> These people are not drunk, as you suppose, since it is only the third hour of the day. But this is what was

uttered through the prophet Joel: "'And in the last days it shall be, God declares, that I will pour out my Spirit on all flesh, and your sons and your daughters shall prophesy, and your young men shall see visions, and your old men shall dream dreams; even on my male servants and female servants in those days I will pour out my Spirit, and they shall prophesy (Acts 2:15–18—quoting Joel 2:28–29).

This prophecy from Joel is just as much for you and me as it was for the early disciples. The manifestation and gifts of the Holy Spirit are for all believers—and for all time. Like every other thing we receive from heaven, these spiritual gifts are received by faith and activated by corresponding action.

I was incredibly fortunate to have a father who was hungry for the things of God. He and my mother were baptized in the Holy Spirit in the late 1960s during the charismatic movement. Only a few years later, at the age of seven, I attended a multi-week course called the Life in the Spirit seminar. At the end of this course, everyone had the opportunity to have the leadership pray for them to receive the baptism in the Holy Spirit. The leaders prayed over me to receive the infilling of the Holy Spirit—and I immediately started praying in tongues.

I have continued to pray in tongues throughout my life, and many years later, I experienced the amazing miracle of glossolalia. I was working at the Christian Broadcasting Network at the time, and we were privileged to have Marilyn Hickey as a guest speaker for chapel one day. Marilyn taught on the baptism in the Holy Spirit and speaking in tongues that day. Toward the end of the service, she explained the gift of tongues could be received by faith. She invited us all to pray in tongues together and encouraged those who had not yet received this gift to step out in faith to begin praying in the spirit.

At her invitation, I joined with my coworkers in praying in tongues for a couple moments. When we were done, Marilyn encouraged everyone to continue praying in tongues as the Holy Spirit led and then dismissed the meeting. I turned to leave and was stopped by one of my students from Regent University and her sister. These two young ladies were from the nation of Jordan and were attending the university together.

My student approached with wide eyes and asked if I knew what I was saying as I prayed. I smiled and replied, "No, I was just praying in the Spirit as I have done since I was a child." The two sisters looked at each other in unbelief then turned back to me. "We heard you praising Almighty God in perfect royal Arabic," they told me.

The wonderful thing about this story is it produced another beautiful result. Up to this time, these two young students did not believe that the gifts of the Spirit were active in our modern day. Now they had heard with their own ears praise to God in Arabic from someone who never spoke the language. Only a few weeks later, my student's sister met a man who had been raised like me in a charismatic household where the gifts of the spirit were in practice. Prior to her experience with glossolalia, she would have never been open to dating a charismatic Christian. But now she accepted his invitation to date. They are now happily married with a growing family and serving together in ministry.

Peter, Paul, Mary, and the Gifts

Now that you are aware that the gifts of the Spirit are for every believer and they can be received by faith, the Peter, Paul, and Mary principle has kicked into action in your life—whether you've realized it or not. So, how will you respond to God's invitation to go to a higher level in your walk with him and your ministry to the world using the gifts of the spirit?

As you ponder this question, it's fascinating to note that all three of the central characters in this principle of faith operated in the gifts of the spirit.

Peter

We've already shown how Peter spoke in tongues on the day of Pentecost. Many other signs and wonders were regularly done among the people by the hands of Peter and the apostles. People carried the sick out into the streets and laid them on cots and mats so as Peter walked by, his shadow fell on some of them, and they were healed. (Acts 5:12, 15, ESV) Peter also moved mightily in the other gifts of the Spirit including word of knowledge (Acts 5:8-9); healing the lame man at the temple (Acts 3:5-6); receiving prophetic dreams (Acts 10); and even raising Tabitha from the dead (Acts 9:36-40).

Paul

More than anyone else, the apostle Paul explained the phenomenon of the manifestation of the Holy Spirit through his writing and also demonstrated the gifts in his ministry. We see Paul caused the sorcerer, Elymas, to be blind (Acts 13:11); healed the lame man in Lystra (Acts 14:10); cast the demon out of the fortune-teller (Acts 16:18); and raised the young man Eutychus from the dead (Acts 20:9-10).

God was performing extraordinary miracles by the hands of Paul, so that handkerchiefs or aprons were even carried from his body to the sick, and the diseases left them, and the evil spirits went out (Acts 19:11-12).

Mary

Sometimes the Holy Spirit will tuck a small mention of something or someone in the Bible you might miss if you're not reading carefully. Through a quick note from Luke, the writer of the book of Acts, the Holy Spirit makes sure that we know Mary, the mother of Jesus, was in the upper room with the other disciples waiting on the promised Holy Spirit.

In the first chapter of Acts, Luke paints the picture:

> When they had entered the city, they went up to the upper room where they were staying; that is, Peter and John and James and Andrew, Philip and Thomas, Bartholomew and Matthew, James the son of Alphaeus, and Simon the Zealot, and Judas the son of James. All these all were continually devoting themselves with one mind to prayer, along with the women, and Mary the mother of Jesus, and with His brothers (Acts 1:13–14 NASB).

There is no mention of any changes to the list of people gathered when the day of Pentecost arrived, so it can be inferred that these were some of the people present when the Holy Spirit fell upon the early church. So, it is most likely Mary, the mother of Jesus, was filled with the Holy Spirit on the day of Pentecost and spoke with tongues with the other disciples and apostles.

What Are the Gifts of the Spirit?

Paul provides the following lists of spiritual gifts:

Romans 12:6–8

Prophecy, Serving, Teaching, Exhortation, Giving, Leadership, and Mercy

1 Corinthians 12:8–10

Word of Wisdom, Word of Knowledge, Faith, Gifts of Healings, Miracles, Prophecy, Distinguishing between spirits (or discerning of spirits), Tongues, and Interpretation of Tongues

1 Corinthians 12:28–30

Apostle, Prophet, Teacher, Miracles, Kinds of Healings, Helps, Administration, and Tongues

Then there are what some theologians call "the ascension gifts," which Paul distinguishes from the gifts of the Holy Spirit when he quotes the psalmist:

> When He ascended on high, He led captive the captives, and He gave gifts to people (Ephesians 4:8 NASB, quoting Psalm 68:18).

Many believe these gifts are extensions of the ministry of Jesus and are therefore in a different category, holding different authority. Another distinguishing factor of these gifts is that they are meant to equip believers to do the work of preaching the Good News and fulfilling the Great Commission. Like the other gifts, those called to an ascension gift office operate in that place by faith.

I Wish Dad Was Here

When I teach on the gifts of the Spirit, I sometimes tell the story of my friend who was injured while playing a game called wallyball, which is volleyball played in a racquetball court. Jumping to make a play, he came down with his full weight on a twisted foot. He immediately fell to the ground in tremendous pain. His ankle instantly swelled up and he thought he had broken a bone.

Now, if I believed that the gifts passed away with the death of the apostle John on the Isle of Patmos—I would have just told my friend I was sorry he was hurt and hoped he felt better soon.

If I believed that Christians only received one spiritual gift, then I would have been equally unable to help, as my primary gift is prophecy. I might have replied sadly, "If only my dad was here, he could pray for you because his primary spiritual gift is healing."

What happened is everyone gathered around my friend, and I led a prayer for the complete healing of this injury. Two of the guys helped him up and walked him to the car as he limped painfully along. The next day, I watched as he walked into the office with barely a limp—no crutches, no cast, and barely any pain. I asked him what happened, and he said the pain got less and less as they drove to the urgent care facility. Then by morning, it was only a slight annoyance. He smiled and said, "God healed me."

How could that happen—since I don't have the gift of healing? In Mark 16:18, Jesus said, "they [believers] will lay hands on the sick, and they will recover." He doesn't say "believers with the gift of healing"—he just says "believers."

Going back to the prophecy of Joel quoted by Peter on the day of Pentecost—the promise is that "I will pour out my Spirit on ALL flesh." The Hebrew words used are *kol*, which means "all", and *basar*, which means flesh or mankind. If you are a human being, then you qualify to receive this gift of the Holy Spirit.

Jesus made this astounding statement to his disciples:

"I tell you the truth, anyone who *believes in me* will *do the same works* I have done, and even greater works, because I am going to be with the Father." (John 14:12 NLT, italics and emphasis added)

It couldn't be clearer than that—the manifestation of the Holy Spirit is available to all who believe. I believe the Bible is telling us the Holy Spirit distributes the gifts we need when they are needed. Some may be more gifted in certain manifestations—but all believers can move in all the gifts as they are needed for God's purpose. It's like a professional baseball team. Some players are gifted in certain positions, or as hitters, or as pitchers, but all can play any position if called upon by the coach.

THE GIFTS OF THE SPIRIT AND THE PETER, PAUL, AND MARY PRINCIPLE

Considering this amazing promise, let's review the PP&M checklist to see the pattern.

A. God has initiated the communication by promising through Jesus the Holy Spirit would give each New Testament believer "power to be his witnesses" (Acts 1:8) and by the Old Testament prophet Joel the Spirit would be poured out on all flesh;
B. Many people are filled with the fear at the thought of being used by God in a supernatural way through the manifestation of the spirit;
C. God always brings his peace. Paul writes this remarkable passage to the church in Philippi: "Keep putting into practice all you learned and received from me—everything you heard from me and saw me doing. Then *the God of peace will be with you*" (Philippians 4:9 NLT, italics and emphasis added). As you DO what God calls you to do in the way he wants you to do it—which is revealed in Scripture—then you will be filled with his peace.
D. In this natural world, we can sometimes wonder if God has really promised that we can move in the supernatural gifts of the Spirit. It's helpful to remember we are God's hands, feet, and voice on the earth. As colaborers with God, we work together to take the gospel to every person on the earth. As Jesus promised, the infilling of the Holy Spirit empowers us to be his witnesses to those lost in darkness.
E. God calls us to the higher level in our walk with him which turns our gaze from our own self-interest to an outward focus. This selflessness reflects the first and second commandments working together—to love the Lord your God with all your heart soul mind and strength and to love your neighbor as your love yourself.
F. We must decide if we will step out in faith, allowing God to use us to touch the lives of others through the gifts of the Spirit.

G. Once a decision is made, there must be corresponding action, taking the experience from the spiritual into the natural realm. If you see someone hurting, ask if you can pray for their healing. If you sense God leading you to share a word of encouragement with someone, step out in boldness, knowing God is with you.
H. When you act in faith, moving out in the gifts of the Spirit, the grace of God comes on the scene, mixing with his promise to pour out his Spirit on all flesh, and then wonderful miracles take place as the Holy Spirit manifests himself to bring healing and freedom.

The gifts of the Holy Spirit are wonderful tools we can use to be witnesses in the earth today. Now that you know these gifts are available to you, I encourage you to walk through the steps of the Peter, Paul, and Mary principle and enter this amazing world of wonder. A tremendous adventure awaits as you step out further in faith and love for God and other people.

—CHAPTER THIRTEEN—
FAITH FOR THE FUTURE

Political upheaval, COVID and the threat of other pandemics, climate change, the possibility of nuclear war or nuclear accidents, broken families, the heroin and opioid crisis, the threat of technical tyranny, the possibility of global financial collapse—it's undeniable, we live in a fallen world with monumental problems. In this new millennium, we face major challenges requiring ingenuity, diplomacy, cooperation, wisdom, and peaceful solutions. Today, more than ever, we need godly women and men who will walk in faith, listen for God's voice, and move in the power of the Holy Spirit.

This is nothing new. In every generation, God has raised up people of faith to bring answers to pressing problems.

Isaac Newton: While Newton sought to explain the secrets of the universe, he did so guided by faith in a loving creator. "This most beautiful system of the sun, planets, and comets could only proceed from the counsel and dominion of an intelligent and powerful Being. ... This Being governs all things."[1]

William Wilberforce: By the eighteenth century, many people in England had rejected the church. William Wilberforce wanted to draw people back to Christian faith—

but he didn't want that experience to merely include church attendance. He desired people to walk out their faith in tangible ways, to take the gospel into all British society. He didn't only desire social reform, but he wanted to change the way people thought of virtue and how it affects everyday life.

Wilberforce and his supporters attempted to bring answers to every social ill in the country. He worked to help the poor find work and the necessities of life. He worked to establish educational reform, prison reform, health care reform, and to limit the number of hours children were required to work in factories. Wilberforce was a leading member of the Clapham Sect, a group of evangelical Anglican Christians who desired to attempt massive social improvements. Together, they worked for the abolition of the slave trade and promoted missionary work around the world. Their efforts led to the ending of the British slave trade and to the formation in 1824 of the Society for the Prevention of Cruelty to Animals—among many other accomplishments.[2]

Charles Dickens: Though Dickens was a critic of the elite in the Church of England, he embraced the biblical message of caring for the poor and loving thy neighbor. In addition to being a prophetic voice against injustice in his day—a gift that continues to echo in our world today—Dickens' final book was called *The Life of Our Lord*. He wrote the book so his children would become familiar with Jesus Christ, and he read it to them often. "I put a New Testament among your books," he wrote to one of his children, "because it is the best book that ever was or will be known in the world."[3]

Harriet Beecher Stowe: According to her daughter, when Harriet, a member of the famous Christian Beecher family, visited the White House, President Abraham Lincoln is reported to have greeted the author of *Uncle*

Tom's Cabin with the words, "Is this the little woman who made this great war?" Stowe's book opened the eyes to many about the harsh conditions faced by slaves, stirring the controversy over slavery, and helping many to see it as an evil institution.[4]

George Washington Carver: In 1941, *Time* magazine called George Washington Carver a genius in the vein of Leonardo da Vinci. As an inventor and agricultural scientist, Carver revolutionized farming in the south after the Civil War through the cultivation of soil-enriching crops, such as peanuts and soybeans, from depleted cotton soil. He discovered more than a hundred uses for the sweet potato and three hundred uses for the peanut.

Carver proved that one could have a deep faith in both God and science. In pursuing his study of science, Carver would ask God to lead him. In 1920, while speaking to the Young Men's Christian Association in Blue Ridge, North Carolina, he explained how his discoveries about the peanut were made:

> Years ago I went into my laboratory and said, "Dear Mr. Creator, please tell me what the universe was made for?" The Great Creator answered, "You want to know too much for that little mind of yours. Ask for something more your size, little man." Then I asked, "Please, Mr. Creator, tell me what man was made for." Again, the Great Creator replied, "You are still asking too much. Cut down on the extent and improve the intent." So then I asked, "Please, Mr. Creator, will you tell me why the peanut was made?" "That's better, but even then it's infinite. What do you want to know about the peanut?"

Carver described how God began to show him how to use the peanut to bless mankind. "And then the Great Creator taught me to take the peanut apart and put it together again. And out of the process have come forth all these products!"[5]

Susan B. Anthony: The Anthony family was Quaker, with a long history of social justice and anti-slavery activism. Susan B. Anthony dedicated her life to woman's rights and suffrage, having learned the traits of fairness and justice in her godly family. She raised up the banner for the abolition of slavery, the right of women to own property and to attend institutions of higher learning, and the right of women to vote. Anthony resisted the pressure to secularize the women's moment, "knowing it would take both the religious and the irreligious to change society."[6]

Martin Luther King, Jr.: The civil rights movement in America was led almost exclusively by people of faith who were living out what they believed in tangible ways. The primary leader of this movement was a second-generation Baptist minister named Martin Luther King Jr. In a 1955 address at Holt Street Baptist Church in Montgomery, Alabama, King intertwined his faith and biblical passages with the cause of civil rights. "We are not wrong, we are not wrong in what we are doing. If we are wrong, the Supreme Court of this nation is wrong. If we are wrong, the Constitution of the United States is wrong. And if we are wrong, God Almighty is wrong. If we are wrong, Jesus of Nazareth was merely a utopian dreamer that never came down to Earth. If we are wrong, justice is a lie, love has no meaning. And we are determined here in Montgomery to work and fight until justice runs down like water, and righteousness like a mighty stream."[7]

His famous letter from Birmingham Jail is considered by people around the world to be one of the most important moral treatises of the twentieth century. In justifying the civil disobedience he advocated in the face of segregation, he wrote: "How does one determine whether a law is just or unjust? A just law is a man-made code that squares with the moral law or the law of God. An unjust law is a code that is out of harmony with the moral law. To put it in the terms of St. Thomas Aquinas: 'An unjust law is a human law that is not rooted in eternal law and natural law. Any law that uplifts human personality is just. Any law that degrades human personality is unjust.'"[8]

It was the persistent drumbeat of this moral message, combined with prayer, action, nonviolent resistance and, when necessary, civil disobedience that moved the hearts and minds of people across America and around the world. King and many thousands of devout believers lived out their faith in tangible ways and pulled answers from heaven to earth to bring justice to the oppressed during the civil rights movement.

You are no different than any of these men and women. All are created equal in the image of God. There is no greater or lesser in the eyes of our creator. The old saying is true: the ground is level at the foot of the cross. Everyone is born with God's plan already programmed into them. The psalmist declares:

> You saw me before I was born. Every day of my life was recorded in your book. Every moment was laid out before a single day had passed. (Psalm 139:16 NLT)

God has a wonderful plan for your life. He has prepared you with talents, abilities, and personality to see that plan accomplished—for your good, for the nurture and care of your family, and for his plan to reach lost souls with the gospel. Paul gives us two important concepts along these lines. First, we are preprogrammed by God to do good works—not to attain salvation, but to display it as a reflection of God's love.

> For we are his workmanship, created in Christ Jesus for good works, which God prepared beforehand, that we should walk in them. (Ephesians 2:10)

Secondly—and this is one of the most amazing and important concepts in the New Testament—as disciples of Jesus Christ, we are also created to be "ambassadors" and "ministers of reconciliation," representing God and making his message known in the earth.

> All this is from God, who through Christ reconciled us to himself and gave us the ministry of reconciliation; that is, in Christ God was reconciling the world to himself, not counting their trespasses against them, and entrusting to us the message of reconciliation. Therefore, we are ambassadors for Christ, God making his appeal through us. We implore you on behalf of Christ, be reconciled to God. (2 Corinthians 5:18–20)

Now that you know the Peter, Paul, and Mary principle, and realize you are part of God's plan to reconcile the lost world to himself, the next task must be to discover what that calling may be. What is your Peter, Paul, and Mary moment?

KEEPING IT IN BALANCE

As I wrote earlier, one thing that became clear very quickly when I was a hospital chaplain was our faith does not always influence God's will. God is sovereign, and his plan will always be accomplished. Our plan may or may not line up with his, so as we stand in faith, we must do so with humility. The great evangelist Corrie ten Boom—who survived imprisonment during World War II yet lost several family members to the Nazis—spoke of this to Pastor Chuck Swindoll. "You must learn to hold everything loosely … Even your dear family. Why? Because the Father may wish to take one of them back to Himself, and when He does, it will hurt you if He must pry your fingers loose."[9]

The writer of Hebrews gives us what some theologians have called "the hall of fame of faith" in chapter 11. The first verses define the concept of faith and then gives a list of those who triumphed in their witness for God in the earth. The chapter speaks of the great faith and the corresponding great deeds of Abel, Enoch, Noah, Abraham, Sarah, Isaac, Jacob, Joseph, Moses, Rahab, Gideon, Barak, Samson, Jephthah, David, and Samuel—"Who through faith conquered kingdoms, enforced justice, obtained promises, stopped the mouths of lions, quenched the power of fire, escaped the edge of the sword, were made strong out of weakness, became mighty in war, put foreign armies to flight" (Hebrews 11:33-34).

But then, the writer shows that in this world, some who put action to their faith suffer from the inhumanity of their fellow humans. That list includes people like Catherine of Alexandria, Jan Huss, Dietrich Bonhoeffer, Martin Luther King, Jr., or Jesus Christ himself.

> Some were tortured, refusing to accept release, so that they might rise again to a better life. Others suffered mocking and flogging, and even chains and imprisonment. They were stoned, they were sawn in two, they were killed with the sword. They went about in skins of sheep and goats, destitute, afflicted, mistreated—of whom the world was not worthy (Hebrews 11:35-38).

We must always remember God will answer our prayers in his way and in his time. All the people healed by Jesus eventually died—and so will we. The final healing is in heaven or when Jesus returns.

On the other hand, God *wants* to use you and me to share his love, grace, wisdom, and strength with hurting people who are lost in darkness. But someone must go to tell them. Paul asks the Roman church these vitally important questions:

> But how can they call on him to save them unless they believe in him? And how can they believe in him if they have never heard about him? And how can they hear about him unless someone tells them? (Romans 10:14 NLT)

Will you be like Isaiah the prophet?

> And I heard the voice of the Lord saying, "Whom shall I send, and who will go for us?" Then I said, "Here I am! Send me." (Isaiah 6:8)

Know this, if you surrender to Jesus, follow the leading of the Holy Spirit, and act on your faith in the manner of the Peter, Paul, and Mary principle, you will see wonders beyond what you can likely imagine at this point.

KNOWING OUR AUTHORITY IN CHRIST

Those who follow the call of God quickly recognize their dependency on him—which leads to a growing prayer life. When we pray, the Bible says we are to come humbly into God's presence to make our requests known to the Lord (Philippians 4:6). We need to be walking in a proper relationship with the Lord as we enter his presence. As Pat Robertson often says, "Keep short accounts with God." As we enter a time of prayer, we need to repent for any sin, known or unknown, and we need to forgive anyone who has offended us in any way.

We are entering the throne room of the living God, the book of Hebrews tells us, by a new and living way, by the blood of Jesus, the Lamb of God (Hebrews 10:19–23). We are addressing the Creator of the Universe—the omnipotent, omnipresent, omniscient God. He is all-powerful. That is why Peter, Paul, and Mary all trembled during their supernatural encounters. We too must show proper respect and reverence.

Having said that, it's also important to observe some other biblical instructions we have concerning prayer. Even though God is the King of kings, and all-powerful, he is also a loving Father, and we can trust his goodness. The apostle James declares:

> Whatever is good and perfect is a gift coming down to us from God our Father, who created all the lights in the heavens. He never changes or casts a shifting shadow. (James 1:17 NLT)

WAR IN THE HEAVENS

We don't enter his presence lightly—both out of reverence, but also from an awareness of spiritual warfare. Paul warns us in his letter to the Ephesians that when we say yes to God's plan for our lives, we enter a spiritual battle.

> For we are not fighting against flesh-and-blood enemies, but against evil rulers and authorities of the unseen world, against mighty powers in this dark world, and against evil spirits in the heavenly places. (Ephesians 6:12 NLT)

As we have shared, Paul implores us to put on the full armor of God and to wield the sword of the Spirit. Paul is not just speaking symbolically. These military metaphors represent the real battle raging in the spirit realm. On a few occasions in the Bible, the Lord allows us to see behind this spiritual curtain to witness angelic skirmishes in the heavens. In the Old Testament, we are told the prophet Daniel had a troubling vision in the third year of Cyrus the king of Persia (Daniel 10).

Daniel didn't understand the meaning of this disturbing revelation, so he began a time of fasting and prayer. Many days passed before he was given the interpretation of what he had seen. God opened Daniel's eyes to see a vision of a man clothed in linen, his face like the appearance of lightning, and the sound of his words like the voice of a multitude.

Understandably, Daniel was left trembling and on his knees. The man addressed him, "O Daniel, man greatly loved, understand the words that I speak to you, and stand upright, for I have now been sent to you."

The angel explained the delay in answering Daniel's prayer.

> Then he said to me, "Do not be afraid, Daniel, [sound familiar] for from the first day that you set your heart on understanding this and on humbling yourself before your God, your words were heard, and I have come in response to your words. But the prince of the kingdom of Persia was standing in my way for twenty-one days; then behold, Michael, one of the chief princes, came to help me, for I had been left there with the kings of Persia. (Daniel 10:12–13 NASB, bracketed comment added)

This angel of the Lord was sent to help Daniel understand the heavenly vision. If Daniel had not persisted in prayer—which is a matter of faith—he might not have received the message from God. Many Christians make the mistake of giving up too soon in prayer. They don't recognize the spiritual warfare that rages in the spirit realm and that our prayers of faith can have a tremendous impact. The Bible gives us this promise about our prayers:

> The earnest prayer of a righteous person has great power and produces wonderful results. (James 5:16 NLT)

God's people are often ineffective, unprotected, and suffering lack because they either don't understand spiritual warfare, or they choose to not believe in it.

We see another example of the hidden legions of God's army in an Old Testament account when the king of Syria was making war against Israel. This monarch was greatly troubled at how Elisha was foiling his strategies by supernaturally revealing his battle plans to the king of Israel (2 Kings 6). So, the Syrian king sent a great army with horses and chariots to surround the city where Elisha was staying. When Elisha's servant went out to the city gates in the morning, he saw that the town was under siege. In a panic, he flew to Elisha's house and cried out, "My master, what shall we do?"

Calmly the great prophet of God replied:

> Do not be afraid, for those who are with us are more than those who are with them." (2 Kings 6:16 NASB)

No doubt the servant was perplexed at this answer. It was plain to anyone with eyes the Syrians greatly outnumbered them. But Elisha was not looking at the situation merely through human eyes. He was seeing through the eyes of faith—and he was about to give his servant a very special gift. Looking up to heaven, Elisha declared, "Lord, I pray, open his eyes that he may see."

The Lord opened the eyes of the young man, and he saw a sight that must have sent him immediately to his knees. There before him, the mountain was full of horses and chariots of fire all around the city. So, when the Syrians came down to him, Elisha prayed to the Lord and said, "Strike these people, I pray, with blindness." Instantly the entire army was blinded. With no choice, they helplessly followed Elisha right into the stronghold of the king of Israel. Elisha prayed again for the Lord to open their eyes. When their sight returned, they recognized they were surrounded by the army of Israel. Elisha showed mercy on these poor fellows and spared their lives. After ordering the king to feed the entire army, he sent them back to their masters—a strong demonstration of the power of God.

We need to realize that the realm of the spirit is real. Spiritual warfare is real. We have a real spiritual enemy—Satan, a thief who seeks to steal, kill, and destroy (John 10:10). He behaves like a roaring lion, seeking whom he may devour (1 Peter 5:8). But we are assured by God's promise that we have his protection:

> We use God's mighty weapons, not worldly weapons, to knock down the strongholds of human reasoning and to destroy false arguments. (2 Corinthians 10:4 NLT)

Why would Paul tell us about our spiritual armor and weapons if we weren't called upon to use them?

The truth is we are not only required by God to use them, but we are also called to wield them in faith.

Let's remember God gave "dominion" or "authority" to humankind in Eden. We have a certain level of authority on the earth merely because we are of the race of humans. But when we're a born-again Christian, we have also been given a measure of supernatural authority because of our position in Christ. The authority we possess takes a quantum leap forward when we're baptized in the Holy Spirit—filled with God's power for witnessing.

We see a dramatic example of this when Jesus sent out seventy-two of his disciples to minister in his name (Luke 10). He dispatched them two-by-two into every city he was about to enter. He instructed them, "Heal the sick, and say to them, 'The kingdom of God has come near to you.' He who hears you hears Me, he who rejects you rejects Me, and he who rejects Me rejects Him who sent me" (Luke 10:9, 16). Can you see how intertwined we are with Christ—when people reject the message that we bring in his name, God considers that they are rejecting him, not us.

In other words, God's got our backs. That should give us great boldness in preaching the gospel to the lost.

Soon the disciples returned to him with joy reporting, "Lord, even the demons are subject to us in Your name!" The reply Jesus gives is interesting, and in context, enlightening regarding our position in him. He tells them, "I saw Satan fall like lightning from heaven. Behold, I give you the authority to trample on serpents and scorpions, and over all the power of the enemy, and nothing shall by any means hurt you. Nevertheless, do not rejoice in this, that the spirits are subject to you, but rather rejoice because your names are written in heaven" (Luke 10:18–20).

Jesus explicitly tells the disciples that Satan and his minions are subject to believers because of the authority we receive from God when we are in Christ. The same authority Jesus gave to his disciples was then extended to all who believed on him and received the baptism in the Holy Spirit in the book of Acts. Now that authority is available to you and I as joint heirs with Jesus Christ (Romans 8:17).

Why On Earth Do I Exist?

The apostle John tells us in his first epistle, "The reason the Son of God appeared was to destroy the works of the devil" (1 John 3:8). As followers of Christ, we are a part of God's plan to destroy the devil's work in the earth and bring freedom to the captives held in bondage to sin.

Did you ever wonder why God didn't bring an end to Satan's kingdom after Jesus's death and resurrection? Why are we still here? After all, Jesus said, "It is finished" (John 19:30). The apostle Peter gives us a clue in his sermon after he healed the leper at the gate of the temple in the book of Acts.

> But what God foretold by the mouth of all the prophets, that his Christ would suffer, he thus fulfilled. Repent therefore, and turn back, that your sins may be blotted out, that times of refreshing may come from the presence

of the Lord, and that he may send the Christ appointed for you, Jesus, whom heaven must receive until the time for restoring all the things about which God spoke by the mouth of his holy prophets long ago. (Acts 3:18–21)

God is bringing about the restoration of all things in Christ and he has chosen to do it in part through his church. That, I believe, is one of the reasons we are still here.

The other reason is this life is our preparation for eternity. God has given most of us seventy to one hundred years on this planet. But we will spend all of eternity with him in heaven. We are learning how to walk in faith while we are here—and I believe we will continue to walk in faith for all of eternity.

The Bible tells us God has ordained for the saints to rule and reign with him (Revelation 5:10; Daniel 7:27; 1 Corinthians 6:1–3; 2 Timothy 2:12). The Bible doesn't explicitly tell us how we will be involved in ruling—only that we will be ruling "with Christ."

Someone once said that this life is "training for reigning."

Paul tells us Jesus Christ is the head of the church, and we as believers make up his body. Since all things are placed under Jesus, and we are his body, then all dominion is under our feet when we are in Christ. That fact is made abundantly clear when he declares to the Romans, "I want you to be wise as to what is good and innocent as to what is evil. The God of peace will soon crush Satan *under your feet*." (Romans 16:19–20, italics and emphasis added).

Remember, the feet are part of the body. Jesus as the head is directing his body to crush the head of the serpent. As part of the body of Christ, then, we are working in covenant with God to bring all dominion and principality and power under the Lordship of Jesus Christ. This will fulfill the original messianic prophecy that God declared to Adam and Eve that the seed of man shall bruise the head of the serpent (Gen 3:15).

Planting Seeds of Faith

It was an understanding of this authority in Christ that made Peter, Paul, and Mary the great leaders of the faith they became. But their walk with Christ all started out with a mustard seed-sized encounter where they chose to believe what God told them.

You can begin such a journey of faith today.

Once we understand the authority given to us in Christ, we can step out in boldness, knowing God is with us and he is for us. We don't have to live out our lives as timid, fearful people clinging to dry and dead forms of religion. We can take our rightful place as joint heirs with Jesus Christ, boldly declaring to the principalities and powers, "I know my God. I am strong. I will do exploits" (Daniel 11:32).

Jesus taught this concept to his disciples:

> When a strong man, fully armed, guards his own palace, his goods are safe; but when one stronger than he attacks him and overcomes him, he takes away his armor in which he trusted and divides his spoil. (Luke 11:21–22)

This is what God is calling us to do to Satan and his kingdom. Jesus defeated Satan on Calvary:

> In this way, he disarmed the spiritual rulers and authorities. He shamed them publicly by his victory over them on the cross. (Colossians 2:15 NLT)

Now He is calling his followers to conduct a "search and destroy operation" against the forces of evil while we are on this earth. That is exactly what the church faces today in defeating Satan and his hordes. The top dog, Lucifer, was soundly defeated when Jesus died on the cross and rose from the dead. Paul writes to the Colossian church: "In this way, he disarmed the spiritual rulers and authorities. He shamed them publicly by his victory over them on the cross." (Colossians 2:15, NLT)

It is true that Satan is still active on planet earth, but his doom is certain and he knows it. As Larry Tomczack has said, "He may be alive, but he's not doing well. If fact, he knows his time is short."[9] Satan knows that you're a part of an end-time army that co-laboring with Christ to bring about his ultimate defeat. Now we, the army of God, are cleaning out the nests of demons who are holding on in the earth.

The Bible tells us that in the end days Satan will launch a last-ditch counter offensive. It will be ugly, but again he will be utterly crushed by Christ and his followers.

After Peter declared in front of the other disciples that Jesus was the Christ, the Son of the living God, Jesus commended him saying, "You are Peter, and on this rock I will build my church, and the gates of hell shall not prevail against it. I will give you the keys of the kingdom of heaven, and whatever you bind on earth shall be bound in heaven, and whatever you loose on earth shall be loosed in heaven" (Matthew 16:18–19).

The Lord has given every believer this same ministry of binding and loosing—it was not just for Peter in his day, and it is not just for the professional ministers of today. This is a mighty weapon in the spirit realm to be used in submission to the Lordship of Jesus Christ, with humility toward heaven, and boldness toward the kingdom of darkness.

Jesus explained this warfare in the spirit realm: "From the days of John the Baptist until now the kingdom of heaven has suffered violence, and the violent take it by force" (Matthew 11:12). God wants us to be mighty in him, pulling down strongholds, declaring that the kingdom of God has come. Like John the Baptist before us, God is raising up an end-time company who are declaring to principalities and powers—both seen and unseen—"prepare ye the way of the Lord. Jesus is coming soon!"

THE DISCIPLES WERE LIKE US

Peter, Paul, and Mary were three fallible human beings, just like you and me. They only became mighty by dying to themselves and allowing God to live through them.

Peter made multiple mistakes and suffered continually of "foot in mouth disease"—often saying the wrong thing at the wrong time.

Saul set out to persecute, jail, and even kill, followers of Jesus. Even after giving his life to Jesus, Paul could sometimes be a bit difficult. Things got so heated between Paul and Barnabas they parted ways and didn't work together again.

Despite some who would say Mary was without sin—not a biblical concept, by the way—Mary herself admitted to her need for a Savior:

> My soul magnifies the Lord, and my spirit rejoices in God my Savior. (Luke 1:46–47)

Like all sons of Adam and daughters of Eve, Mary inherited the sin nature. "For all have sinned and fall short of the glory of God" (Romans 3:23), and "There is none righteous, no, not one" (Romans 3:10).

Let's not forget that Simon Peter rejected Jesus at his greatest time of need, denying him three times. After his resurrection, Jesus displayed his compassion to Peter when he recreated the dramatic events that first brought the two of them together. Young John, who witnessed both these events, recorded this tender, yet supernatural compassionate encounter.

After Jesus rose from the dead, he appeared to the disciples several times in different locations. In John 21, we see the story of how one early morning, just after the dawn, Jesus appeared on the shore of the Sea of Galilee to greet Peter, John, and some other disciples after their unsuccessful night fishing trip.

The previous evening, Peter declared to the others he was going fishing. Now this seasoned fisherman wasn't talking about dropping a line in the water with a worm and a hook. Peter headed for his trusty boat, the same one that Jesus had stood in as he taught the crowd three years earlier. He planned to do some serious fishing, hoping for a serious catch. Now you don't head out into the water with this type of rig unless you plan to sell your catch when you return.

So, when Peter said, "I'm going fishing," I believe he meant, "I'm going back to my fishing business."

The three-year adventure with Jesus had been exciting, stimulating, exhilarating, and sometimes frightening, but I believe Peter was now convinced it was not a lifestyle he could continue. He had let Jesus down—big time. He'd shot off his big mouth, like he had often done before, only now he didn't have the courage or the character to follow through on his grandiose promises.

"I would even die with you, Jesus." The words played again and again in his mind—as did those other damning words, "Jesus? I don't even know the man." Simon Peter was sure he was no longer of any use to Jesus or his kingdom, especially now that he was the risen Christ.

But Jesus had other plans for this broken vessel.

When the morning had come, Jesus stood on the shore, but the disciples didn't recognize Him. Shouting across the misty surface of the calm sea, Jesus asked, "Children, do you have any food?"—as if he didn't already know.

The disciples may have thought this was a potential customer, wanting to buy some of their catch. Dejectedly, they called back, "No, we have not had any luck tonight."

Jesus hollered back to them over the rippling waves, "Cast the net on the right side of the boat, and you will find some."

"Oh no, not another shoreline expert," Peter may have thought. Yet something was strangely familiar about this scenario. Exchanging curious glances, the disciples wondered if they should follow the advice of this stranger. One by one they turned to look at their foreman, the crusty old salt who had led them through these many years. He was tired. He was frustrated with the unrewarded toil from the previous night. Peter was still in turmoil over his rejection of Jesus in the garden of Caiaphas, the high priest. But something told him it was worth one more cast of the net.

Each man grabbed a portion of the net and at Peter's signal they heaved it into the sea. Suddenly, the surface of the water was alive with flopping, fluttering, fabulous fish—their silver bodies glimmering in the early-morning sun. Instinct took over, and the veteran fishermen tugged in tandem, straining every muscle to pull in the bulging nets. Try as they may, they were not able to heave the enormous catch into the boat.

When you've failed God; when you have rejected his guidance; when you have walked away from the only being in the universe with the words of life—at those times, it is sometimes difficult to recognize God is at work in your life. Even when God recreates a life-changing moment to capture our attention, sometimes it takes one of our friends to show us the fingerprints of the Savior.

Young John turned to Simon and declared, "It is the Lord!"

As if scales had fallen from his eyes, Peter turned and suddenly recognized Jesus as well. He pulled on his outer garment and dove into the sea, swimming with all his might toward the Savior.

By the time the rest of the disciples had dragged the net full of fish to shore, Jesus had built a fire and was cooking some fish and warming some bread. "Bring some of the fish you have just caught," he directed. Peter sprang into action, dragging the net bulging with large fish to the shore. Even though there were so many, the net was not broken.

Jesus invited the disciples to eat and served them bread and the fish. When they finished their breakfast, Jesus turned to Peter and shocked him with this question: "Simon, son of Jonah, do you love me?"

With sadness in his heart, Peter answered truthfully, "Yes, Lord; you know that I love you."

Jesus responded with the simple words of restoration, "Feed my lambs."

A second and a third time Jesus asked the piercing question, "Simon, son of Jonah, do you love me?"—one time for every denial. By the third time, Peter was overcome with grief. Jesus was God in the flesh. Even though in that horrible moment of weakness he had denied even knowing him, Peter knew Jesus could read his heart. Jesus was God, and he knew Peter really did love him. With tears in his eyes, he replied, "Lord, you know all things; you know that I love you."

Jesus looked deep into his eyes and with compassion, said again, "Feed my sheep." The call to follow him was still as valid on that shore as it had been on a similar shore three years before.

You may have never experienced restoration like Peter did. Instead, you may be like Paul, a confident young professional with goals and ambitions that drive you. You may have been a religious person, maybe even a religious leader. But one day, God toppled you from your high horse. You may be facing the question, "What now, God?" It took several years of God working in the life of Paul before he was ready to go back out into the world as his servant. If you have been zealous for the Lord, if you have desired to be used in mighty ways for his kingdom purposes, don't be weary in well doing. Keep pressing forward in Him.

Many years after his miraculous conversion, Paul stood in chains on trial before King Agrippa and declared, "I was not disobedient to the heavenly vision" (Act 26:19). Though his life was difficult and full of peril, Paul continued the journey begun on that Damascus road—a sojourn that led him around the ancient world, preaching the gospel to peasants and kings, finally completing his assignment of faith in a Roman dungeon.

What Are You Believing For?

What has God promised to you? What is the heavenly vision for your life? Have you had an encounter with God where he has declared his will to you? Then respond like Peter, Paul, and Mary and receive the promises of God in faith.

If you are a born-again Christian, then the Scripture declares all the promises of God are yours to claim. You are a child of the King. God always causes you to prosper in him—and that is not only talking about money, but also the other riches of life like a loving family, peace, and joy. You are a part of a royal priesthood, a chosen generation, a holy people. You are the apple of God's eye. You need to see yourself the way God sees you.

What are you believing for? What is it that you need in your life? If you know God has promised it to you, either in Scripture, or directly to your heart or through a prophetic word or godly counsel—and if you have an enduring peace about that direction—then stand firm in the promises of God.

We live in perilous times. The future of the world depends on Christians understanding the principles of faith and walking in them. So, who will you be? It is up to you to decide to pull those promises into the natural realm by faith and corresponding action. God is eagerly waiting to bless you and bless the world through you.

Like Peter, Paul, and Mary will you respond in faith? A lost and dying world is yearning to hear from you—and a great adventure awaits.

ABOUT THE AUTHOR

From webcasts to television and radio, and from conferences and churches to boardrooms, Dr. Craig von Buseck has been in the public eye for more than thirty-five years. As a sought-after keynote speaker, he has spoken across the US and overseas. Craig is an award-winning, multi-published author and serves as the Digital Content Manager for the Parenting section of FocusontheFamily.com in Colorado Springs, Colorado. He is also a contributing writer for CBN.com, The Write Conversation, MTL Magazine, and Charisma Magazine. He holds a Doctor of Ministry and an MA in Journalism from Regent University.

Craig's most recent books are *Victor! The Final Battle of Ulysses S. Grant*, which is a biography of the last two years in Grant's life, and a companion book, *Forward! The Leadership Principles of Ulysses S. Grant*.

Craig's recent book, *I Am Cyrus: Harry S. Truman and the Rebirth of Israel*, won the prestigious Selah award for nonfiction and was a finalist for The Truman Award from the Harry S. Truman Presidential Library. Craig's other books include *Nobody Knows: The Harry T. Burleigh Story*, *NetCasters: Using the Internet to Make Fishers of Men*, and *Praying the News*, cowritten by 700 Club cohost Wendy Griffith.

Craig has extensive speaking experience and travels often to conferences, professional events, churches, and writer training meetings.

https://vonbuseck.com
https://facebook.com/craigvonbuseck
https://youtube.com/channel/UC4XngihXgoXse2Jrr4N5LpQ
https://twitter.com/craigvonbuseck
https://amazon.com/Craig-Von-Buseck/e/B001K8JB1U/ref=ntt_dp_epwbk_0
https://instagram.com/buseckcraigvon/
https://bookbub.com/profile/craig-von-buseck
https://mewe.com/i/craigvon_buseck

ENDNOTES

Chapter Two
1. *Star Wars: Episode IV—A New Hope*, written and directed by George Lucas, (1977, 20th Century Fox), motion picture.

Chapter Four
1. *The Nativity Story*, directed by Catherine Hardwicke (2006; Temple Hill Entertainment/New Line Cinema), DVD.

Chapter Five
1. Williams, Dr. J. Rodman. "Theology Q&A - Christ." CBN.com Spiritual Life. https://www1.cbn.com/biblestudy/theology-q%26a-christ.
2. Gilbert, Dr. Daniel, (theologian) in discussion with the author, September, 2022.

Chapter Six
1. Larry Tomczak, *Biblical Declarations to Build Your Faith*, read by Larry Tomczak, Cleveland, Ohio. Larry Tomczak Ministries, 1980, audio recording.

Chapter Eight
1. Bill Hamon, *Prophets and Personal Prophecy* (Shippensburg, PA: Destiny Image Publishers, 1987), 32.

Chapter Eleven
1. Shakespeare, William. 'Hamlet'. Sparknotes. https://

www.sparknotes.com/nofear/shakespeare/hamlet/act-3-scene-3/.

2. Heinrich August Wilhelm Meyer, *Heinrich August Wilhelm Meyer's NT Commentary*. (Hannover, Germany: Translated from the Sixth Edition of the German by Rev. Peter Christie, The Translation Revised and Edited by Frederick Crombie, D.D., Professor of Biblical Criticism, St. Mary's College, St. Andrews, Edinburgh. T. & T. Clark, Edinburgh, Scotland) 1880. https://biblehub.com/commentaries/acts/17-28.htm.

3. F.W. Pitt, "The Maker of the Universe," Thinking On Scripture (blog), March 12, 2022, https://thinkingonscripture.com/2014/06/06/the-maker-of-the-universe-f-w-pitt.

Chapter Thirteen

1. Isaac Newton, *The General Scholium to Principia Mathematica*, 1687 (P3) https://inters.org/Newton-Scholium-Principia-Mathematica.

2. "William Wilberforce," Religions, BBC, last updated July 5, 2011, https://www.bbc.co.uk/religion/religions/christianity/people/williamwilberforce_1.shtml

3. Charles Dickens, *The Life of Our Lord*. Wikipedia. https://en.wikipedia.org/wiki/The_Life_of_Our_Lord.

4. Annie Fields, *Authors and Friends* (New York: Houghton Mifflin, 1896), 181. https://books.google.com/

5. Tim Moore, "Life Lessons from a Christian Exemplar: George Washington Carver." Rapture Forums, November 12, 20221. https://www.raptureforums.com/forums/threads/life-lessons-from-a-christian-exemplar-george-washington-carver.185047/.

6. "People and Ideas: Confronting Modernity/Progressive Era," American Experience, PBS, https://www.pbs.org/wgbh/americanexperience/features/godinamerica-modernity-progressive/.

7. "10 Famous Quotes from Dr. Martin Luther King, Jr.," Constitution Daily, National Constitution Center, https://constitutioncenter.org/blog/10-famous-quotes-from-dr-martin-luther-king-jr-2

8. Martin Luther King, Jr., "An Unjust Law is No Law At All: Excerpts from "Letter From Birmingham Jail." Intercollegiate Studies Institute. https://isi.org/intercollegiate-review/an-unjust-law-is-no-law-at-all-excerpts-from-letter-from-birmingham-jail/. Accessed August, 2022.

9. Chuck Swindoll, "Holding on Loosely," Insight.org, April 11, 2013, https://insight.org/resources/article-library/individual/holding-on-loosely.

10. Larry Tomczak, *Biblical Declarations to Build Your Faith*, read by Larry Tomczak, Cleveland, Ohio. Larry Tomczak Ministries, 1980, audio recording.

www.ingramcontent.com/pod-product-compliance
Lightning Source LLC
Chambersburg PA
CBHW062219080426
42734CB00010B/1952